Henry Allen Tupper, First Baptist Church

The first century of the First Baptist Church of Richmond, Virginia.

1780-1880

Henry Allen Tupper, First Baptist Church

The first century of the First Baptist Church of Richmond, Virginia. 1780-1880

ISBN/EAN: 9783337261009

Printed in Europe, USA, Canada, Australia, Japan

Cover: Foto ©Lupo / pixelio.de

More available books at **www.hansebooks.com**

THE FIRST CENTURY

OF

The First Baptist Church

OF

RICHMOND, VIRGINIA.

1780-1880.

RICHMOND:
CARLTON McCARTHY,
819 Broad Street,
1880.

Entered according to Act of Congress, in the year 1880,
By CARLTON McCARTHY,
in the Office of the Librarian of Congress, at Washington.

To
JAMES THOMAS, Jr.
THIS VOLUME,
MEMORIAL OF THE CHURCH HE LOVES SO
WELL AND SERVES SO LIBERALLY,
IS APPROPRIATELY AND
AFFECTIONATELY
DEDICATED.

The Editor.

CONTENTS.

I.

	PAGE.
INTRODUCTION,	9-39

II.

DISCOURSES, SKETCHES, AND ADDRESSES	41-334
History of the Church, by J. L. Burrows	43-105
Deceased Pastors, by W. D. Thomas	107-139
Houses of Worship	141-152
"House of One Franklin," by W. H. Gwathmey	143
Houses of Worship, by C. Walthall	148
Officers of the Church, by J. B. Watkins	153-172
History of the Sunday-school, by C. Walthall	173-184
Jeter Memorial	185-209
Relation of the Church to Education, by J. L. M. Curry	187
Address, by J. B. Hawthorne	190
The Church in its Relation to Missions, by H. A. Tupper,	211
Origin and History of the First African Church, by Robert Ryland	245
Fraternal Addresses	273-294
By Basil Manly	275
By E. W. Warren	283
By H. McDonald	292
Sermon, by T. T. Eaton	295
Extempore Addresses	319-334
By Thomas Hume, Jr.	321
By W. H. Williams	325
By J. Wm. Jones	330
By J. B. Hawthorne, Pastor	333

III.

SUPPLEMENTARY STATISTICS AND STATEMENTS	335-350
INDEX	351

I.

INTRODUCTION.

BY
H. A. TUPPER.

INTRODUCTION.

THE First Baptist Church of Richmond, Virginia, holds a leading position among the Baptists of the State and of the South. This eminence has been acquired by the number and strength of its membership, the ability and piety of its pastors, the variety and utility of its activities, the unity and conservatism of its spirit, the wide-spread influence it has exerted more or less directly in the counsels of the denomination, and the venerableness of its age crowned with memories of triumphs of grace all through its long conflict of faith. It was fit, therefore, that, with the approach of its one-hundredth anniversary, thoughts should arise of special thank-offerings to the Lord, and of some suitable commemoration of the Divine Goodness and Guidance.

At the first "Conference Meeting" of the

Church in the year 1880, on the evening of the twenty-sixth of January, the following paper, presented by Hon. J. L. M. Curry, LL.D., was adopted as the sentiment of the Church:

> This First Baptist Church of Richmond was organized in 1780, before the Revolutionary War had closed, or the independence of the United States had been acknowledged by Great Britain. Richmond was then a village of less than two thousand inhabitants. The Church was organized, under the pastorship of Rev. Joshua Morris, with fourteen members. From these feeble beginnings, in those dark days, this Church has grown to be one of the largest and most useful Churches in America. It seems meet that we should take a review of the past, thankfully recognize the Father's goodness in our past history, set up our Ebenezer, and "take courage" for new and enlarged activities in the future. Therefore,
>
> *Resolved*, 1. That as a Church we here record our heartfelt gratitude to God for his abundant and continuing mercies, and recognize the duty of newly consecrating ourselves to the work of holding forth the word of life and showing our love in all holy conversation and godliness.
>
> *Resolved*, 2. That a Committee of eleven be appointed, who shall take such steps as may be needful for celebrating by the Church, in a becoming manner, its one hundredth anniversary.

On Wednesday evening, the fourth of February, the Pastor, Rev. J. B. Hawthorne, D. D., announced the names ensuing as the Committee appointed under the Second resolution:

J. L. M. Curry, H. A. Tupper, James Thomas, Jr., R. H. Bosher, A. P. Fox, Wm. G. Dandridge, P. H. Starke, Coleman Wortham, John

C. Williams, R. W. Powers, and Wm. H. Turpin.

On motion of Mr. R. H. Bosher, the Pastor was added to the Committee.

As the result of their deliberations, the Committee reported to the Church, on the twenty-fourth of May, that the eighth and ninth days of June next had been set apart for a Centennial Celebration, which would be utilized for the proposed Jeter-Memorial; and that they had advertised the following Programme—modified by the editor into accord with the actual facts of the occasion :

PROGRAMME.

TUESDAY, 8TH JUNE, 10 A. M.

MUSIC.

READING SCRIPTURES.
By the Pastor, *Rev. J. B. Hawthorne, D. D.*

PRAYER.
By *Rev. H. A. Tupper, D. D.*

MUSIC.

HISTORY OF THE CHURCH.
By *Rev. J. L. Burrows, D. D.*, of Kentucky.

MUSIC.

SKETCHES OF DECEASED PASTORS.
By *Rev. W. D. Thomas, D. D.* of Virginia.

DOXOLOGY.

BENEDICTION.

AFTERNOON SESSION, 4 O'CLOCK.

MUSIC.

READING SCRIPTURES.
By *Rev. B. Manly, D. D.*, of Kentucky

PRAYER.
By *Rev. J. H. Eager*, of Virginia.

MUSIC.

THE HOUSES OF WORSHIP.
By Deacon *C. Walthall.*

MUSIC.

SKETCHES OF OFFICERS.
By *J. B. Watkins, Esq.*

THE SUNDAY-SCHOOL.
By Deacon *C. Walthall.*

ORIGIN AND HISTORY OF THE FIRST AFRICAN CHURCH.
By *Rev. Robert Ryland, D. D.*, of Kentucky.

DOXOLOGY.

BENEDICTION.

NIGHT SESSION, 8 O'CLOCK.

JETER MEMORIAL.

MUSIC.

PRAYER.
By *Rev. E. W. Warren, D. D.*, of Georgia.

MUSIC.

RELATION OF THE CHURCH TO EDUCATION.
By *Hon. J. L. M. Curry, LL. D.* Read by *Dr. Burrows.*

MUSIC.

Address by *Rev J. B. Hawthorne, D. D.*

MUSIC.

Address by *Rev. Wm. E. Hatcher, D.D.* Collection Conducted by *J. L. Burrows, D. D.*

DOXOLOGY.

BENEDICTION.

WEDNESDAY, 9TH JUNE, 10 A. M.

MUSIC.

READING SCRIPTURES.
By *Rev. E. W. Warren, D. D.*

PRAYER.
By *Rev. B. Manly, D. D.*

MUSIC.

THE CHURCH IN ITS RELATION TO MISSIONS.
By *Rev. H. A. Tupper, D. D.*

MUSIC.

FRATERNAL ADDRESSES.
By *Revs. B. Manly, D. D., E. W. Warren, D. D., H. McDonald, D. D.*

DOXOLOGY.

BENEDICTION.

EVENING SERVICE, 8 O'CLOCK.

SERMON.
By *Rev. T. T. Eaton, D. D.*

EXTEMPORE ADDRESSES.

MUSIC BY CHOIR.

DOXOLOGY.

BENEDICTION.

The morning of the eighth of June, 1880, dawned brightly and blandly, as in sympathy with the joyous scenes to be inaugurated by it, and by which itself was to be made a lasting remembrance. At an early hour—perhaps two hours before the appointed time—many persons found their way to the Church. Some were attracted, doubtless, by the rumors of the tasteful floral decorations provided by the ladies. For over the vestibule was wreathed in green and gold: "Constituted 1780." The same, in gold letters, was displayed over the pulpit, between the portraits of Andrew Broaddus, Sr., and J. B. Jeter. The whole front of the rostrum was enclosed and concealed by a deep and conical arrangement of choice plants and flowers —native and exotic—the apex of the cone, or rather its truncation, on a level with the upper line of the speaker's stand. Other adornings were in keeping with this central ornamentation.

The building was soon crowded. The church and community were quick with the spirit of the Celebration. It was to be more than the festivity of a single church or even denomination. In directing public attention to the anticipated anniversary, a city-paper voiced the spirit of the occasion in this language:

The numerous denomination of Christians of whom this Church has been a century plant of wondrous growth and beneficence will take and diffuse a genuine interest in this ensuing memorial of a religious body whose history is almost the history of Richmond. But the interest will by no means be confined to Baptists. For that large catholicity of religious sentiment which pervades the pious people of Richmond will joyously hail an opportunity, such as this, to express itself in fraternal gratulations and gratitude to the good Giver who has preserved and strengthened the weak and tender plant, until, with strong root, towering trunk, and broad branch, it stands an object of moral beauty, and better, a source of moral and spiritual blessings to thousands who have crossed the flood and others who are crossing now. There is scarcely a State in the Union in which there does not live some former member of this illustrious old Church. Her sons and daughters will come from afar to offer thank-offerings for her life and history.

The general interest was deepened by several circumstances:

The Pastor was permeated with the Centennial idea, and dispensed himself "in season and out of season"—in pulpit and parlor; in stores and on the streets; and seemed bent on lifting up the people to his own lofty conception of the occasion.

Rev. J. L. Burrows, D. D., who had been pastor of the Church for twenty years, and was one of the most popular men that ever lived in Richmond, had, the night previous, delivered in the Church a grand lecture on "America's Contribution to the Wealth of the World." The day before that, on Sunday, the sixth of June, the pulpit had been occupied by two other ex-pastors, Rev. Drs. Basil Manly and E. W. Warren. The sermon of the one was elegant and elevating, mellow and melting: that of the other proved the instrument in God's hands of quickening into new life at least one soul—a precious and prayer-begirt daughter of the congregation. Besides, Dr. Robert Ryland—"the noblest Roman of them all"—was among the people who will never cease to lament his quitting the "Old Dominion."

Around each of these men of God clustered associations, tender and sacred. They belonged to different periods of the history of the Church; but each period was represented in the Church and congregation. At their appearance blessed memories came trooping up, and each was invested with peculiarly loving and reverential regard. These generous sympathies moved in circles; but these circles crossed, and blended, and were in perfect harmony, until the forces attracting to the several centres caught and held every member and every family of the Church.

Further, the city had not recovered from the shock of Dr. Jeter's death, and it was commonly understood that some memorial to him would be advocated in the celebration. Finally, the people were in a mood for public gatherings. The General Association of Virginia, held in Petersburg, only twenty miles distant, was just adjourned. Many of our people had attended the inspiriting sessions of that body. Delegates and visitors accompanied, or followed, our citizens to Richmond. This and other company, enlivening many homes with beauty and brilliant talk, kept alive and intensified the social and public sentiment, and added no little to the occasion by the profound personal interest of these almost strangers.

These circumstances all tending to the common end, the first session of the celebration found a grave audience instinct with eager expectation and undisguised enthusiasm.

Punctually at ten o'clock, the choir burst forth in the anthem: "We praise thee, O Lord." With this announcement, Dr. Hawthorne, accompanied by the gentlemen who were to participate in the morning exercises, appears on the platform, like Saul among his brethren. After the music, he holds up an old time-worn Bible, with lower edge literally worn away some half of an inch by the preacher's peculiar habit of *thumbing* while preaching, and says: "This was John Kerr's Bible, which he preached from when Pastor of this Church, fifty years ago." Here was started another current of exciting interest. With sonorous voice, he read from the venerable volume the Ninetieth and Ninety-First Psalms—Scriptures as appropriate as if written for the occasion. After prayer, an old Hymn-book was exhibited, as "the one first used in the present building." The Pastor said: "Some people criticise our modern music. Suppose I 'line out' a hymn that our fathers used to sing from this book, with twenty-one stanzas, and request that the last stanza be repeated!"

Following music—not from the old Hymn-book—Dr. Burrows was introduced as "needing no introduction." His paper, with the other papers, will be duly noticed. After his discourse, Rev. Wm. D. Thomas, D.D., was felicitously presented by Dr. Hawthorne, who, by the way, in introducing speakers, and turning every incident to good account, and in presiding generally over the meetings, excelled himself. As we are touching now merely the incidentals of the celebration, let it be remarked, that the occasional *jeux d'esprit* were delicate and tittilating, and diffused good feeling throughout the audience. At times, the humor was broader, and, as the Psalmist says: "Our mouth was filled with laughter." As suggestive—though only dimly suggestive—of the mild pleasantry that sometimes blended with the beautiful and the pathetic during the Celebration, this item from a report of the *State* is selected :

Dr. Hawthorne said, thirty years ago, when he was a "very little boy," Dr. Manly was called as a pastor to this Church.

Dr. Manly, of Kentucky, said if Dr. Hawthorne was a very little boy thirty years ago, he had grown marvelously since. Somebody had treated him well. He had helped and been instrumental in having the Richmond Female Institute established. Had been its president and teacher. He went there yesterday to see if, in the sweet pupils, there was as much beauty as when he was there. No, he said, *not so much beauty because there were not as many beauties*. The gentle daughters of his pupils he saw. Like another, he felt like weeping and raining tears on the golden tresses of the young maidens he saw, for the sake of their mothers under the sod, whom he had taught. To others beautifully and pathetically he referred.

The afternoon session of the first day was enlivened by the exhibition from the rostrum of a large pencil-sketch of the old church-house on Cary Street, occupied previous to the year 1802, prepared by Mr. George A. Minor, to illustrate the paper of Deacon Walthall on the "Houses of Worship." A similar illustration, on a more extended scale, by the same gentleman, of the "House of one Franklin," where the Church was organized in 1780, was also on hand, but was not presented to the audience, as the paper on that house, by Deacon W. H. Gwathmey, was not quite finished. These pictorial reminders of the humble beginnings of the Church will be committed, it is understood, to the "Historical Society."

Like a General, Dr. Burrows, in conducting the *collection*-part of the "Jeter-Memorial" meeting, with pleasant peremptoriness, ordered Drs. Hawthorne and Warren, with the writer, to "go among the people," which they were "forward to do." The Pastor had said that the Celebration would "culminate" in this session; but, in the glow kindled next morning by the "Fraternal Addresses," he exclaimed: "This is the great day of the feast." At night amid the closing speeches, which he called "declarations of love," he revised again his judgment, affirming this last session "the feast of fat things."

It was greatly regretted that Rev. D. B. Winfree, D. D., who had served the Church most acceptably during Dr. Burrows' engagement in the Memorial work for Richmond College, and whose name was on the original programme, could not be present. Rev. Duncan McGregor, another admired supply of the Church, was on the other side of the ocean. The absence of Dr. Curry in Europe was deplored.

No account of the Celebration could be satisfactory without some notice of the music. Now grand, then exquisite, always inspiring gratitude and praise, it heightened the enthusiasm of the meetings. The choir was composed as follows:

SOPRANOS.
MRS. JACOB REINHARDT.
MISS C. V. WYATT.

ALTO.
MRS. JOHN H. KNOWLES.

TENORS.
MR. EDWARD H. HOFF.
MR. FRANK W. CUNNINGHAM.

BASSES.
MR. U. B. PLEASANTS.
MR. ALEX. ABERNETHY.

ORGANIST AND DIRECTOR.
PROF. JACOB REINHARDT.

As the hymns and tunes of our Fathers interest their children of this age, so the following record may not be uninteresting to our posterity at the close of another century:

FIRST DAY.

MORNING.

1. TE DEUM.—WE PRAISE THEE O LORD.............. *Warren.*
   CHOIR.

2. PALM BRANCHES—(Baritone Solo)...................... *Faure.*
   MR. U. B. PLEASANTS.

3. I KNOW THAT MY REDEEMER LIVETH—(Sop. Solo). *Handel.*
   MRS. JACOB REINHARDT.

4. OLD HUNDRED...
   CHOIR AND CONGREGATION.

AFTERNOON.

1. SOFTLY NOW THE LIGHT OF DAY......................... *Abbott.*
   CHOIR.

2. BE THOU FAITHFUL UNTO DEATH (Tenor Solo.)
   Mendelssohn.
   MR. EDWARD H. HOFF.

3. ONE SWEETLY SOLEMN THOUGHT—(Barit. Solo.) *Ambrose.*
   MR. A. ABERNETHY.

4. OLD HUNDRED ....
   CHOIR AND CONGREGATION.

EVENING.

1. TRIO.—PROTECT US THRO' THE COMING NIGHT.
   Curschman.
   MRS. REINHARDT, MRS. KNOWLES, MR. HOFF.

2. Home of the Soul—(Tenor Solo).....................
    MR. F. W. CUNNINGHAM.

3. Beyond the Smiling and the Weeping............*Bonar.*

4. Old Hundred......................................
    CHOIR AND CONGREGATION.

SECOND DAY.

MORNING.

1. Venite.—O Come, Let Us Sing, etc................*Millard.*
    CHOIR.

2. How Sweetly Flowed the Gospel-Sound.
    Sir J. Bowring.

3. Go Preach the Blest Salvation............*Sidney Dyer.*

4. Old Hundred......................................
    CHOIR AND CONGREGATION.

EVENING.

1. Consider the Lilies—(Soprano Solo)..............*Topliff.*
    MISS C. V. WYATT.

2. If with all your Hearts—(Tenor Solo)...*Mendelssohn.*
    MR. EDWARD HOFF.

3. Blest be the Tie that Binds......................*Fawcett.*

4. Gloria in Excelsis................................*Mozart.*
    CHOIR.

Among the most interested and physically active in the celebration was "Jefferson," who having served the office of Sexton faithfully for many years, deserves here honorable mention; as well as his predecessor, Carter Page, who seemed much like Anna of old, "which departed not from the Temple," and who was so devoted to the very brick and mortar of the Church, that when some extensive changes were made he was overwhelmed with grief, and died, it is said by a physician, of "a broken heart."

Ample accommodations were made for reporters; and the press, secular and religious, furnished elaborate reports of the proceedings.

The two discourses of the first session occupied just three hours. Other papers and addresses also were necessarily long. All the documents are herein published. The editor has thought, however, that some synopsis of them might be of advantage to the reader. With this view, and in order to present a connected narrative of the several sessions, the report of the *Religious Herald*, of the seventeenth of June, with a few needed changes, is here transcribed:

> Rev. J L. Burrows, D. D., of Kentucky, from 1854 to 1874, Pastor of the Church, delivered the first discourse, which was a "Centennial History of the Church." Its delivery occupied nearly two hours; but the author's fine elocution and the intrinsic interest of the paper enchained the undivided attention of the assembly. In alluding to his entrance upon the pasto-

rate with a wife and little children, and leaving it, after twenty years, "a lonely man," family all dead or scattered, and to the death of "devout women not a few," the Doctor's emotion overcame him for a moment, and speaker and people were melted to tears.

The address began with a general view of Virginia's and Richmond's condition in 1780, in relation to politics, population, commerce, agriculture, architecture, and manufactures, the means and rate of travel, etc. Virginia's vast territory, war history, currency, historic names, and fabulous provision prices were vividly recited, and the village of Richmond, with eighteen hundred inhabitants, well described. Brief sketches of early Baptist ministers and churches also preceded the immediate history of the organization and growth of the Church. Fourteen members formed the Church, which met in the house of a Mr. Franklin, on Union Hill, who was, no doubt, a member. The loss of the first record book leaves us in ignorance of the names of the other thirteen. Though unregistered here, their "record is on high." After some moving about, the next place of meeting was between Second and Third Streets, fronting Cary. The third, by the gift of Dr. P. Turpin, was the house of worship erected on the present site of the First African Church, which was abandoned for the spacious edifice now occupied by the Church. In 1790, the membership had increased to 200, in 1824 to 820, and in 1841 to over 2,000, when the colored element withdrew to form the African Church, leaving about 400 white members. Rev. Joshua Morris was pastor from 1780 to 1787, Rev. John Courtney from 1788 to 1824, the date of his death. Rev. John Kerr was pastor from 1825 to 1832, Rev. Isaac Taylor Hinton from 1833 to 1835, Rev. J. B. Jeter from 1836 to 1849, Rev. Basil Manly, Jr., from 1850 to 1854, and Rev. J. L. Burrows as above stated. The salient traits of these men were hastily delineated, as well as those of the co-pastors and pastors *pro tem.*, Keeling, Broaddus, Taylor, Ryland, Jennett, Winfree, Curry, and Tupper. He concluded with a resume, showing that one church of fourteen members in 1780 had swelled to nineteen churches, in Richmond and Manchester, in 1880, numbering 16,847 members. Dr. Burrows ended his address by an appropriate reference to the pastorates of his successors, Drs. Warren and Hawthorne.

Rev. W. D. Thomas, D. D., of Norfolk, reared and baptized in this Church, followed in an admirable address, sketching discriminatingly the "Characters of the Deceased Pastors of the Church." Of Morris, the materials were meagre. Yet, from his career in Kentucky and glimpses of history, it was evident he was a useful, earnest minister of the gospel, though he had few advantages of education. The primitive simplicity, sincere piety, stern truthfulness, and ministerial industry of Courtney, and his John-like tenderness in old age, were happily illustrated by incidents and occasional amusing expressions. The portrayal of John Kerr was striking and life-like. His superb natural gifts of oratory were exemplified by specimens furnished by the ready and retentive memory of the venerable Rev. E. Dodson. The organizing ability and culture of Rev. I. T. Hinton, with his sound and impressive preaching, had due attention. Dr. Thomas then drew a bold and independent picture of Dr. Jeter's character, clearly reflecting his "father in the gospel" as a man, thinker, writer, and preacher. We regret that the limits of this article do not allow details. Dr. Thomas also sketched the characters of Bryce, Broaddus, Keeling, Jennett, etc. His paper was throughout chaste and thoughtful.

At the afternoon session Deacon Christopher Walthall, one of the oldest and best informed members, read two papers—one describing the structures, location, improvements, etc., of the several Houses of Worship, and the other giving a history of the Sunday School in connection with the Church. The probable date of its organization was believed to be 1817, and four teachers and six pupils, perhaps, its initial numbers. The names of the superintendents, some of the teachers, and other interesting facts were given, constituting a mass of information of much value for future use and preservation. General satisfaction was evinced at the manner in which the part assigned Deacon Walthall was performed.

J. B. Watkins, Esq., followed with a fine limning of the Officers of the Church. The earliest known officers, down to the latest departed, were depicted; more length of portraiture given, of course, to those of longest service and widest notoriety. Thus the traits of Clerks Crane and McCarthy, and Deacons Frayser, Winston, Farrar, Reins, Sizer, Thomas, and Crane, were more vividly drawn. The diversified features of the last four were critically analyzed and contrasted, we think justly, and the grateful fact adduced that, while God gives "diversities of gifts, there is the same Spirit." Mr. Watkins' address was carefully prepared and handsomely delivered.

Again, at night, a large congregation filled the Church, and the services were directed in the interest of the "Jeter Memorial."

Rev. Dr. Burrows read an excellent, brief paper, prepared by Dr. J. L. M. Curry, before his departure to Europe, on the "Relation of the Church to Education." It stated that, in 1833, as shown by the minutes, Elder John Kerr, the pastor, was President of the Virginia Education Society, out of which grew the Seminary, and afterwards Richmond College. The Treasurer and five of the Managers were members of this Church. Ever since, the Education Board has had representatives from the Church, and also generous donations, and the College, in its Trustees and Faculty, has depended somewhat on the Church. Efforts for endowment have received from it efficient help, and it is the only Church in the State which has a scholarship in the College for the education of sons of Baptist ministers. Richmond Female Institute has ever found in the Church zealous and liberal friends, patrons, Trustees, and Teachers. The Southern Baptist Theological Seminary has always been the constant recipient of First Church benefactions, in efforts for endowment and support of students and Faculty. Reference was also made to the recognition, on the part of the Church, of the potency of education in moulding and vitalizing man's whole being, and bringing it into accord with the will of God. Allusion was also made to the manifested interest of the Church in the objects of the "Jeter Memorial"—to wit, the providing a hall in the proposed addition to the college building, in which should be deposited, along with his bust or picture, the books and manuscripts bequeathed by Dr. Jeter to the College.

The pastor, Rev. Dr. J. B. Hawthorne, delivered an eloquent address, in which he claimed that gratitude for the great mercies received from the Lord should impel his people to use means in the upbuilding of our College, than which nothing was more vitally important to the progress of a religious denomination and the extension of divine truth. And the interests of the College might be promoted, and a deserved and appropriate monument, at the same time, erected to the memory of Dr. Jeter, one of the most efficient pastors of the Church, by adding another wing to the buildings, with a Hall to be called after the departed veteran. Dr. Hatcher followed in a brief and spirited address, Dr. Burrows conducted the collection, and over $6,000 were subscribed.

On Wednesday morning there was another meeting, at which the Rev. Dr. H. A. Tupper read a summary of an excellent paper he had prepared, detailing the Connection of the Church with Missions during the century. The Doctor delicately declined to use the time needed for its entire reading, that others from a distance might have ample opportunity to be heard.

He divided the Centennial History of the Church into three periods, showing that during the first period, from 1780 to 1813, Joshua Morris and John Courtney were practical friends of Missions, and the Virginia Foreign Missionary Society was organized in this Church in 1813, the first, it is said, south of Philadelphia.

Second period, 1813 to 1846. Luther Rice represented funds of the Church in the General Convention. The Female Missionary Society and the Sewing Society of the Church were organized before 1816. The latter has sometimes given $700 per annum, and the former has given some $11,000. This Church has been the largest contributor to the General Association, and may be called the mother of the Southern Baptist Convention, whose first anniversary was held in this building, and every officer of its Board of Foreign Missions, except three, has been given by this Church.

Third period, 1846 to 1880. The Mite Box Committee of the Woman's Missionary Society of Richmond has raised $1,300, and the Society itself has given over $5,000, the Young Men's Missionary Society has given over $4,000, the Young Ladies' Missionary Society contributes $500 a year, the Dorcas Society is one of the most efficient Missionary Societies of the Church, the Girls' Aid Society is just organized and has raised $17, the infant class of the Sunday-school has given in ten years some $500.

Summary: The Church gives $3,200 per annum to missions. Since 1813 it has given over $60,000. At the close of the next centenary may it be said of her: "She hath done what she could."

The venerated Dr. Robert Ryland of Kentucky, for twenty years pastor of the First (Colored) Baptist Church, read a paper of great clearness and strength, tracing its organization and history, which we propose to publish in full, and, therefore, will not anticipate.

Rev. B. Manly, D. D., Professor in the Southern Baptist Theological Seminary, then delivered an appropriate and pathetic address, recalling reminiscences of his pastorate, and urging enlarged and liberal education and Christian consecration. He was followed by Dr. E. W. Warren, of Georgia, pastor three and a half years, from 1875 to 1879, whose address of fraternal greeting was in the happiest vein. He congratulated the Church on the auspicious occasion, the presence of so many former pastors, etc. Rev. Henry McDonald, D. D., of the Second Church, concluded the session with a fraternal address, full of generous, cordial feeling for the Old Mother Church.

At night, Rev. T. T. Eaton, of Petersburg, delivered an able discourse on the necessity of worthy "*ideals*," based on the text, "Be ye therefore perfect even as your Father in heaven is perfect." The Rev. Thomas Hume, Jr., once a pupil in the Sunday-school, Rev. W. Harrison Williams, of Charlottesville, converted and baptized in the Church, Rev. J. William Jones, D.D., and the Pastor closed the pleasant exercises with addresses of affectionate greeting and farewell, which we regret our space does not allow us to allude to more particularly. Individuals and societies may well pause at long intervals, to review the past and look forward to the future. Thus gratitude is awakened, errors avoided, hope enkindled, and progress quickened.

The various papers read, with a full description of the celebration, will probably be published, we understand, in a permanent form.

Verily "the little one has become a thousand, and a small one a strong nation." May the church membership discard all promptings to pride, derive new inspiration and energy from her thrilling history, "wait on the Lord, renew their strength, mount up with wings as eagles, run and not be weary, walk and not faint."

The frontispiece of this volume suggests the propriety of giving some more minute description of the building where these Centennial services occurred, and of the unusually interesting dedication of it, than will be found in any of the papers to follow. Two days after the celebration, on the eleventh of June, an old communication of 1841 was reprinted in the *Commonwealth* of this city, which meets precisely the demand, and is a document too valuable not to have here a permanent record:

The readers of *The Commonwealth*, who have, doubtless, been deeply interested in the ceremonies which have just occurred at the Centennial celebration of the First Baptist Church of this city, will no doubt read with pleasure a cotemporaneous account of the dedication of the said Church. The account is extracted from the Richmond *Compiler* of October 19, 1841, and is from the pen of the then editor and proprietor of that paper, James A. Cowardin, Esq., at present of the Richmond *Dispatch*:

Among the most interesting events that has occurred in our city for a long time, may be classed the dedication of the magnificent Church just erected, through the munificence of the congregation of the First Baptist Church (of which the Rev. J B. Jeter is pastor) upon Twelfth Street, near the Powhatan House. This pleasing occasion took place last Sunday (October 17, 1841), and attracted one of the largest audiences ever congregated in our city.

The building is of the Doric order, and in all its parts so strictly consonant that it strikes the beholder with admiration. The architect is Mr. Thos. U. Walter, of Philadelphia, who has also furnished the plan for another religious edifice that is to be a superb ornament to our city, viz., the Second Baptist Church. Mr. Walter is the architect of the far-famed Girard College, and this fact will be a guarantee for the truth of the encomium we pass upon the evidences he has given us here of his taste and architectural knowledge. The Church just dedicated is calculated to hold twelve hundred people seated comfortably, but with a little crowding will store away two thousand.

The interior is exceedingly chaste. The colors are white and blue, the white predominating—the pew cushions being blue. The walls are a glassy snow-white, and the mouldings and central ornament of the ceiling are both simple and elegant. The pitch of the ceiling is the very best in accordance with the general symmetry of the interior, and in its adaptation to sound; a whisper from the pulpit can be heard to the extremes of the Church. The galleries are so pitched and graded that the portion of the audience seated in them seems to be brought more effectually within the range of the preacher's address than usual. In most churches, owing to the height or some other cause, the gallery audience seems not to be so much a part of the audience—*i. e.*, upon whom does not devolve, in so great a degree as upon those below, the responsibilities of order and attention to the church services; they are more like "lookers-on in Vienna," and keep up sometimes a little chit-chat and titter among themselves on their own hook; but in this new Church this responsibility is felt, and the discourse of the preacher is shared alike by the audience above and below. This is decidedly an improvement.

The altar is very neat, and the sacred desk is one of the most unique inventions for the purpose we have ever seen. It is simply a desk, raised to a convenient height, and about four or five feet wide, white, with a damask cushion for the Bible to rest upon. It struck us that we had never seen a desk so well adapted to give the best effect to church oratory. It rests upon a broad, carpeted platform that is ascended by a flight of steps at either end. On the right and left of it, and a little in the rear, so as to form a triangle, are two massive Doric pillars, painted white, that give a fine effect. A recess extends back of these columns, the wall of which is ornamented with a large square of blue damask quilled, with a bright star in the centre. In this recess beneath the floor, which is movable, is the baptismal font, where the baptizing will take place in presence of the congregation. This is an invention that will be productive of great convenience, and by which the exposure and disadvantages attending the ceremony which is performed at a distant water-course will be happily avoided. There is a suite of rooms below, which comprise a large and well-arranged Sunday-school and lecture-room, a study for the pastor, and dressing-rooms, to be used on baptismal occasions.

The exterior is of plain stucco, and the building is ornamented with a heavy-looking steeple of moderate height, to which some have objected, but which, nevertheless, appears to be in perfect keeping with the general style of the building. The front has a recess portico, graced by two immense fluted Doric columns, and is reached by a broad flight of granite steps. It has truly an imposing appearance. So much for this noble building, at once an ornament to the city, and an honor to the congregation that built it.

The exercises of the dedication were opened with the anthem, "Before Jehovah's Awful Throne," by an excellent choir, aided with instrumental music. Then a portion of Scripture was read, after which the following hymn, by Doddridge, was sung by the congregation, to Old Hundred, that most inspiring old sacred air, which is always welcome to the ear:

> And will the great, eternal God,
> On earth establish his abode?
> And will he, from his radiant throne,
> Avow our temples for his own?
>
> These walls we to thine honor raise,
> Long may they echo to thy praise,
> And thou, descending, fill the place
> With choicest tokens of thy grace.
>
> Here let the great Redeemer reign
> With all the graces of his train,
> While power divine his word attends,
> To conquer foes and cherish friends.
>
> And on the great decisive day,
> When God the nations shall survey,
> May it before the world appear
> That crowds were born to glory here.

The Rev. George B. Ide, of Philadelphia, then offered up to the Throne of Grace a most appropriate prayer, which was succeeded by the anthem, by the choir, "Be joyful in God, all ye lands."

Rev. Mr. Ide then delivered the dedicatory sermon—his text, "Blessed are they that dwell in thy house"—lxxxiv. Psalm, 4th verse.

Of this sermon we may with truth say that it was happy in its style and peculiarly so in its adaptation to the occasion. It was remarkable for its solid ability, as well as its sublime passages, its bold and striking similes, and the forcible language in which it was conveyed. We thought there was something decidedly Websterian in the latter feature of the sermon.

The reverend gentleman entered at large into the influences of the sanctuary upon society in all its ramifications—intellectual, political, social, and moral. The attention of the audience enchained throughout, was, perhaps, deepest with regard to the discussion of the influence of religion upon the body politic; its agency in enlightening public judgment, the necessity of a correct public sentiment to the maintenance and enforcement of just laws, and the impotency of laws, however wise, not so sustained. The politician might have learned from this part of the sermon the value to set upon the salutary influences of religion; how necessary they are to give efficiency to his measures for the preservation of peace and order, and the maintenance of a just equilibrium between the different powers of our free and happy Government, and how a corrupt public sentiment and depraved and vicious passions, unrestrained by the precepts of virtue, and unchecked by the enlightened view of the duty of man to his Maker and his fellow, imparted by true religion, would break down all the restraints of order, peace, and justice, and whelm the land with the greatest curses that can be visited upon a nation.

An intensely interesting portion of the sermon to the members, was the picture, we may call it, drawn of the happiness, the consolations, social enjoyments and endearments, and the refreshing and soul-purifying effects of the sanctuary, where men come up in the light of the holy effluence, to meet one another in a capacity from which the cares and vexations of life are shut out, and where the feelings and thoughts are elevated above this scene of life to higher objects—where man looks on himself as a spiritual being—*the heir of eternity*—and has his soul ennobled, enlarged, and enlightened, drawn away from the contentions of this fleeting existence of a few years, to the contemplation of the higher destiny in that better country, for which man is fitted and which he may secure if he will.

After such a picture, the heart was filled with deep emotions at the presentation of its opposite, of the desolation that must prevail where there is no sanctuary, and where the inspiring peals of the church-going bells are never heard.

The reverend gentleman concluded with a touching appeal to the unreligious part of his audience. He threw into this the bright fire of feeling, and disdaining the restraints of written words, uttered a thrilling peroration, which must have made a deep impression. His concluding words were an exhortation to be prepared for the long account and escape that bitter taunt, "Ye knew your duty, but ye did it not."

Rev. Mr. Jeter offered up a feeling prayer, and the ceremonies were closed with another anthem and the benediction.

Thus ended the dedication services of this fine church. Long may its works survive the mutation of time, and when time shall be no more—

> "May it before the world appear
> That crowds were born to glory there."

The next communication explains itself, and the connection of the writer with this memorial volume:

FIRST BAPTIST CHURCH,
Richmond, Va., June 28, 1880.

To H. A. TUPPER, D. D., *1002 Capitol Street*, City.

DEAR SIR: At the regular business-meeting of the Church, held this evening, the following resolution offered by Mr. R. H. Bosher was adopted:

Resolved, That Rev. H. A. Tupper, D. D., be requested to collect, arrange, and edit the papers read, and the addresses delivered, at our Centennial Anniversary; and, that he be authorized to have the same published.

[*Copied from the Minutes.*]

D. O. DAVIS, *Church Clerk.*

Acquiescing in the above request of his Church, which has a right to every service that he can properly render to it, the undersigned, having given a sketch of the occasion which called forth the papers, now presents the papers themselves, in the order in which they were delivered, and in as near their original forms as is consistent with the arrangement and object of the work. He has inserted the paper on the "Franklin House," to which reference has been made; and appended "Supplementary Statistics and Statements," which seemed important to complete the historic view of the Church.

The book is commended to the Church, the Christian public, and the grace of God. Should it prove helpful to the Church in perpetuating the impulse received at the Celebration to a grander future; or, in stimulating other churches, or a single soul, to a higher and broader Christian life, the preparation of the volume for publication will receive a superabundant reward.

RICHMOND, VA., *July 26th*, 1880.   H. A. TUPPER.

II.

DISCOURSES,

SKETCHES AND ADDRESSES.

HISTORY OF THE CHURCH.

BY J. L. BURROWS.

HISTORICAL DISCOURSE.
1780-1880.

A BRIEF general view of the condition of Virginia and Richmond in 1780 will be helpful in apprehending the circumstances under which this First Baptist Church was organized.

In population, political influence, and commercial enterprise, Virginia was the foremost Colony of the thirteen. Yet this most populous of the States had only about five-hundred thousand inhabitants, of whom one-half were blacks, although its territory extended westward and northwestward to the Pacific Ocean and to the great lakes. A few of the landed proprietors had comfortable, some of them elegant, residences, the brick, flooring, and furniture of which were imported from England. The homes of the farmers and laborers were structures of logs, sometimes hewn, oftener in their primitive rough-roundness, the intervals between the logs chinked with loose rock, and daubed with mortar, with huge stone chimneys and pine log fires. The floors were often laid with hewn puncheons or formed of the original soil, leveled or rammed. The kitchens were separate structures, out in the yard.

The full dress of gentlemen included satin short trousers, fastened at the knee, long silk stockings, low quarter shoes with silver buckles; and on the streets, fair top boots, bag wigs, terminating behind in a ribbon-bound queue, and cocked hats.

The agricultural implements were of the rudest kind. The "bull tongue plough," with wooden mould-board, sometimes sheathed with sheet iron, and sometimes with a short wrought iron coulter, was the best until Thomas Jefferson, ten years later, and after several years of study and experiment, invented one more serviceable. The grain crops were sown broadcast, reaped with sickles or scythes, threshed with flails or by the trampling feet of oxen, winnowed by flapping a blanket to raise a breeze against the uptossed grain to drive off the chaff. Three men could reap, bind, and shock an acre of wheat a day, and by extra hard work an acre and a half. Lumber was sawn in pits by two men, the despotic "boss sawer" mounted on the log jerking the long saw up, which his subordinate beneath jerked down again. Cotton and wool were raised in small quantities for domestic use, carded by hand, spun on treadle wheels, woven on hand looms, dyed in butternut or oak bark, cut out and made up by the women of the household.

Travelers rode on horseback, a few in carriages, and a few in stage coaches on the main routes. The swift couriers that bore the news of Cornwallis' surrender, in 1781, from Yorktown to the Continental Congress in Philadelphia, made the journey in the unprecedented time of five days (Oct. 19th to 23d,) and in thirty-seven days (Oct. 19th to Nov. 25th,) the news reached England by the way of France.

The manufactories of Virginia were blacksmiths' shops, and, at wide distances, grist and saw mills, with slowly revolving overshot wheels, on some of the upland streams.

The year 1780 was one of the gloomiest years of the Revolutionary War. Washington in New Jersey was holding back the British forces concentrated in New York City. Arnold's treason had created consternation and doubt in the hearts of the people. The British and Tory forces under Cornwallis had overrun Georgia and South Carolina, and were now in North Carolina burning, plundering, massacring the people, and confiscating their property; and though temporarily checked at King's Mountain, Oct. 6th, and harassed by the onslaughts of Marion, Sumter, Pickens, and Harry Lee, they were driving Generals Green and Gates before them, and steadily advancing into Virginia. Recruits for the army were raised with difficulty; provisions and clothing for the army, in scanty supplies, could only by most strenuous measures be collected or forwarded; and the Continental money was of even less value than Confederate money in 1865.

Among the Acts passed by the Legislature in that year, was one calling out twenty-five hundred militia men, to aid in repelling Cornwallis' army, marching toward Virginia. The number was portioned among the several counties, of which Henrico County was required to furnish eighty three, Hanover one hundred and thirty-five, and Bedford two hundred and two; indicating the relative population of the several counties. An Act, too, was passed for supplying clothing, in which each county was assessed for a certain number of suits, one pair of overalls, two pairs of stockings, one pair of shoes, one wool, fur, or felt hat or leather cap. Each county was required to furnish a definite number of these suits—thus, Henrico, fifty-five; Caroline, ninety-three; Amelia, one hundred and twelve. They were to be collected by distress warrants as taxes. As the women had to spin, weave, dye, and make them up in their homes, they must have had a busy time in that year. Each district was assessed, also, one beef, three hundred pounds, net weight, one wagon and four horses with a driver. Provisions seized by commissioners for the army were to be paid for at the following rates: Wheat, $66⅔ per bushel; corn, $20; peas, $30; oats, $15; pickled beef, $8 per pound; bacon $20 per pound; salt pork, $12; brandy, $60 per gallon; whiskey, $40; West India rum, $80; white biscuit, $300 per hundred weight; ship bread, $200; fine flour, $200; seconds, or ship stuff, $150 per hundred weight. Some of us, remember prices comparing well with these in 1864.

In 1780, Acts were passed dividing Kentucky County into three counties, viz. Jefferson, Fayette, and Lincoln, which comprised what is now the whole State of Kentucky; and for establishing the town of Louisville at the Falls of the Ohio, on one thousand acres of land, forfeited property of one John Connolly, and providing that $30 per acre, if the land sold for so much, should be paid into the Treasury of this Commonwealth. In 1780, the grounds for the public square, upon which to erect the Capitol and Governor's house, were set apart on Shockoe Hill, and streets ordered to be opened, "whether straight or curved," for "communicating with the streets above the brow and below the foot of each hill."

The most important Act of the Assembly in 1780 was one authorizing Dissenting Ministers to celebrate the rites of marriage, and declaring all previous marriages by them legal and valid, and allowing them a fee of "twenty-five pounds of tobacco, and no more," for each marriage-ceremony. The battle for religious liberty had been fought, and this was the almost final surrender of the State-forces to the warriors for soul-freedom. Joshua Morris could now receive and bless the wedding vows of members of his congregation, without liability to legal penalties, in the first year of his pastorate of this Church.

In 1780, the only preacher regularly officiating in Richmond, of whom I can find any trace, was Joshua Morris. This was the only organized Church in the town, if we except the Parish Church of St. John, which was without any resident rector, and had service only at long intervals. The small rear section of the present building on Church Hill was the only church-edifice in the village. Five years later (in 1785) the first meeting of the Episcopal parishioners was held, and a vestry appointed for St. John's Church, who elected Rev. John Buchanon rector. That he very seldom officiated in the Church is clearly indicated in the following extract from a letter written by Mrs. Colonel Edward Carrington to a friend in London, in the year 1792, as quoted in Bishop Meade's "Old Churches," etc.:

"We have not left in our extensive State three churches that are decently supported. Our metropolis even would be left destitute of this blessing, but for the kind offices of our friend Buchanon, whom you remember well as an inmate of our family. He, from sheer benevolence, continues to preach in our Capitol to what we now call the New School—that is to say, a set of modern philosophers, who merely attend because they know not what else to do with themselves. But blessed be God, in spite of the enlightened, as they call themselves, and in spite of Godwin, Paine, and others, we still, *at times*, and particularly on our great church-days, repair with a choice few, to our old Church on the hill (St. John's) and by contributing our mite, endeavor to preserve the religion of our fathers. Delightful hours we sometimes pass there."

In 1780, as we learn from Tucker's Life of Jefferson, Richmond was but a village containing scarcely eighteen hundred inhabitants, half of whom were slaves. It had been designated the seat of government only the year before, 1779, after a lively competition with Hanovertown—the question being decided by a majority of one.

An Act of the General Assembly, in 1780, provided for laying out the streets of the town, connecting, by passable roads up the steep hills, what is now Main Street with Broad Street, setting apart the rugged grounds upon which the Capitol now stands, for the government buildings. The General Assembly met in a large one-story, wooden structure, at the foot of Council Chamber Hill. Mordecai says: "On Fourteenth, or Pearl Street, below Exchange Alley, where Mr. Fry has erected some fine stores" (page 53). Howe says: "The old Capitol, which was private property, stood on the site which is now occupied by the Custom House and some of the adjacent buildings" (page 305). Perhaps, as he wrote in 1845, he refers to an older Custom House, before the present edifice was built. Antiquarians must decide.

Mrs. Colonel Carrington thus humorously limns a picture of the village about this time:

> "It is, indeed, a lovely situation, and may at some future period be a great city; but at present it will afford scarce one comfort of life. With the exception of two or three families, this little town is made up of Scotch factors, who inhabit small tenements here and there, from the river to the hill, some of which looking—as Colonel Marshall (afterwards Judge Marshall) observes—as if the poor Caledonians had brought their houses over on their backs, the weaker of whom were glad to stop at the bottom of the hill; others, a little stronger, proceeded higher; while a few of the stoutest and boldest reached the summit, which, once accomplished, affords a situation beautiful and picturesque. One of these hardy Scots has thought proper to vacate his little dwelling on the hill; and, though our whole family can scarcely stand up all together in it, my father has determined to rent it as the only decent tenement on the hill."—*Meade*, vol. 1, p. 140.

It is to be regretted that the earliest Record Book of the Church has been lost. If intelligently kept, it enrolled the names of the fourteen disciples who entered into the organization. We might trace the influence of their piety upon their descendants, some of whom, it may be, are still living among us. They were probably in humble positions in society, little known beyond their own circle. The names of multitudes of saints—godly and useful—are nowhere recorded save in the "Lamb's Book of Life." But they sowed a few seeds, from which successive and ever-increasing harvests have sprung. They put a little leaven in the mass, which has been working for a hundred years. Who can foretell what grand results may flow from little causes?

We know one name, at least, of the fourteen, Mr. Franklin, of Union Hill. He or his wife—perhaps both—were probably constituent members, as the earliest meetings were held at their house. Researches now going on may discover others of "the fourteen."

From the lost Record Book we should probably have learned, too, what ministers were present to recognize and give fellowship to the new Church. The organization of a Church in the chief town of the State must have been regarded with deep interest by those zealous and laborious preachers who were willing to endure severe persecutions for the advancement of the kingdom of Christ. And in those days of traveling ministers, when many of them almost lived on horseback, it is highly probable that some were here. It may help us to gain some just idea of the character of the men, and of the condition of the churches in the Colony, if we conjecture who among the neighboring and accessible ministers might have been invited to the Council of constitution.

The nearest resident Pastor, in 1880, was *William Webber*, of Dover Church, Goochland County, eighteen miles north of the city. He was one of the heroes who preached Christ's gospel so effectively from the windows of Chesterfield and Middlesex jails. He was a wise and godly man, a leader among those who planned and labored to secure freedom of conscience in this State. He was afterward Chairman of the Committee of Correspondence, and for fourteen years Moderator of the Dover Association.

His nearest neighbor was Pastor of the Goochland Church, twenty two miles from the city, the venerable *Reuben Ford*, converted under the preaching of George Whitefield, the founder and apostle of the Goochland County churches, a prudent, dignified, and laborious servant of Christ, prominent in the counsels of the denomination, in the conflicts for religious liberty, and a very respectable writer.

In Hanover County lived *John Clay*—the father of Henry Clay—and then Pastor of

Chickahominy Church, a plain, but sincere and devout man of God.

There were at that time several traveling evangelists, who were holding meetings and organizing churches throughout this region. Among them, *Elijah Baker*, through whose labors five of the churches in the Peninsula between James and York Rivers were gathered, and seven of the churches on the Eastern Shore; for which services he was rewarded by imprisonment in Accomac jail, and forcibly carried into a vessel to be transported from the country; and *Joseph Anthony*, often associated with Baker in evangelistic work, and who gave some emphatic testimony, and gained some precious experiences, in Chesterfield jail. Either of these might have been present.

Another of these traveling evangelists then in the vicinity was the shrewd, witty, but devoted and indefatigable *John Leland*, whose field of preaching, he tells us, was from Orange down to York," and who passed over that route from November, 1779, to July, 1780, and baptized one hundred and thirty-six converts on that journey. He, doubtless, passed through Richmond, and was within call.

Daniel Marshall, though seventy-four years old in 1780, had yet four years' quite active labor before him, and was ready to go wherever an opportunity of preaching Christ offered. He was one of the Connecticut converts, in the great revival under the preaching of Whitefield; started as a Missionary to the Indians on the Upper Susquehanna; preached his way down into Virginia; became associated with *Shubael Stearns*, his brother in law, only four years dead; ranged into the Carolinas and Georgia, and was now living just over the North Carolina line. The *Murphy boys*, now old men—and *Dutton Lane* were still bearing the fiery cross over the valleys and mountains, and gathering the consecrated clan for the battles of Jehovah.

But to return to the more settled ministers of 1780: there were in the territory now occupied by the Dover Association, *John Courtney*, Pastor of Upper College Church in William County, afterward for thirty six years Pastor of this Church. *Theoderick Noel* of Upper King and Queen Church, an impassioned exhorter, of wonderful power, and who baptized, says Andrew Broaddus, as many converts as any other preacher then in Virginia. *John Wright* was Pastor of Grafton Church. He was called by Semple, "a blessed man of God, faithful to occupy his talents, whose vineyard, though small, was well kept."

John Young was Pastor of Reed's, in Caroline, for six months, and prisoner in Caroline jail. His funeral sermon John Courtney preached in 1817—when he had numbered fourscore years, less one.

Robert Ware, one of the prisoners of King and Queen jail, was now Pastor of Lower King and Queen Church. A man of moderate abilities, but of unquestioned piety and zeal. *James Greenwood*, another of these prison-graduates, who was dragged from his rustic pulpit to finish his interrupted sermon in Middlesex jail, was Pastor of Piscataway Church, in Essex County, a humble, godly, and beloved minister of Christ.

If they desired on so interesting an occasion the services of the most eloquent and popular preacher in Virginia, they had only to send over the Rappahannock and call for *Lewis Lunsford*, now Pastor of Moratico, in the Northern Neck, who had been arrested and threatened with prison, and who was sorry he did not go, rather than allow himself to be persuaded to give security not to preach again in an adjoining county without a license from the Court, which license he failed to procure. But in 1880 their laws could be no longer enforced.

If they looked across the James into Chesterfield for helps, there were *Eleazer Clay,* of Chesterfield Church, an influential and useful man, who lived to be ninety years old. *Wm. Hickman,* of Skinquarter Church, converted during the glorious revival under the walls of Chesterfield jail, who preached his first sermon in Harrodsburg, Kentucky, being commanded and licensed to preach by Thomas Tinsley, and who returned only for a brief time to Virginia, and was now Pastor at Skinquarter; but who soon went back to his beloved Kentucky, where he became one of the honored Patriarchs of that State, who baptized five hundred converts at the Forks of Elkhorn, and lived to the eighty-fourth year of his age.

Jeremiah Hatcher, afterward of Bedford County, progenitor of a long line of preachers —may the number never be less—was Pastor of Tomahawk Church in 1780. These men all lived within a dozen miles of Richmond.

A little further off were *David Tinsley,* of Powhatan Church, whom his persecutors tried to suffocate with fumes of tobacco and red peppers in his Chesterfield dungeon. *Jeremiah*

Walker, of Nottaway Church, of whom Semple says: "few men did more good in so short a time than Walker did round about Nottaway."

James Shelburne, of Lunenburg County, of whom Dr. Alexander said, after hearing his Christian experience and becoming quite intimate with him: "When the old millwright had finished his narrative, I felt much more inclined to doubt my own call to the ministry, rather than that of Shelburne."

John Weatherford, of Charlotte, whose name is immortalized by his bold proclamation of the gospel from behind the high fence which was erected to hide the jail window, which was his pulpit, from the crowds outside in Chesterfield, and whose most eloquent eulogy was written by the venerable Dr. Plummer, who knew him in his old age. He was a frequent delegate to the General Assembly, during the struggle for religious liberty, and was for several years clerk of the General Committee.

John Williams, a man of liberal education for the times, a member of the General Committee, several times a delegate to the General Assembly with petitions for religious liberty, an earnest advocate and planner for ministerial education, a far-seeing and progressive man, was pastor of Meherrin Church in Lunenburg County.

A little farther west, in Pittsylvania, lived *Samuel Harris*, "a Paul among the churches;" and so like one that he was actually elected a sort of Diocesan Bishop with the title Apostle by the misguided enthusiasm and confidence of the General Association. He was undoubtedly a man of superior ability and of great influence. He was once, in Orange County, dragged by the hair from his out-door pulpit, tried and condemned by an Orthodox Court.

Rene Chastaine, the influential and beloved Pastor of Buckingham Church for fifty-three years—from 1772 to 1825—was within easy traveling distance. He was sent for to baptize the converts of the Chesterfield-jail revival. Under threat of prosecution, he gathered the converts together in an arbor, and bravely preached to them and a crowd of the ungodly in the vicinity of the prison.

If the Richmond brethren looked over the field now occupied by the Goshen Association, there were two famous men, who never spared themselves when any good work was going forward, and who were here if they were invited and had not some other godly enterprise on hand; for they seemed nearly ubiquitous.—*John Waller*, who, in his younger days, had been known as the "Devil's Adjutant" and "swearing Jack Waller;" and who now as a minister of Christ was flashing like a brilliant meteor over the State, though frequently eclipsed, having been darkened in the dungeons of four different jails for one hundred and thirteen days in all; who gathered eighteen churches, and baptized over two thousand converts, and was now living in Spottsylvania County. *Lewis Craig*, who took lessons in practical theology in Spottsylvania and Caroline Counties' jails, was now also Pastor in Spottsylvania, and in the following year led most of the members, as an organized traveling church in the wilderness, across the Allegheny Mountains into Kentucky, and settled them on the Elkhorn River, where he died, aged eighty-seven years. *Elijah Craig*, his brother, prisoner in Culpeper and Orange jails, was Pastor of Blue Run in Orange.

Ambrose Dudley was also now in Spottsylvania, but soon after removed to Kentucky, and whose memory is cherished there as one of the fathers of the Elkhorn Association, and afterward, alas! of the Licking Anti-Missionary Association.

John Taylor lived in Fauquier, in 1780, and was a sort of missionary evangelist on the western frontiers, and, in 1783, settled in Woodford County, Kentucky, where, in his old age, he wrote a history of the ten churches with which he had been connected. He was a wise leader in our Kentucky Zion, and preached from his twenty-first to his eighty-first year.

James Garnett, for fifty-five years Pastor of Crooked Run, Culpeper County, where he preached every Lord's Day, declining all calls to a plurality pastorate—if his good example had been generally followed, we should have now a different state of things in our Southern country—could have been here at the organization.

John Pickett, of the Fauquier prison, and founder of six of the old Culpeper Association churches, had his home in Fauquier.

The Fristoes, Daniel and William, of Stafford, soundly Calvinistic, and apostles of the Ketockton Association.

Wm. Marshall, uncle of the Chief Justice, was one of the fashionable aristocracy of Fauquier, and after his conversion and induction into the ministry, was only kept out of jail by the interposition of his Episcopal brother, Col.

Thomas Marshall. During this year, 1780, he migrated to Kentucky, where many of his honored descendants still live.

Richard Major, one of the most useful and godly ministers of that age, was Pastor of Bull Run Church, in Fauquier.

David Thomas, then Pastor of Broad Run Church, in Fauquier County, was perhaps the best educated and most intelligent of all these Fathers of the churches. He was in the vigor of manhood in 1780, and was proclaiming the gospel through the northern counties and into the Southern Neck. He too removed to Kentucky, and labored effectively for many years.

James Ireland, a Scotchman, whom the fanatics of the Established Church tried to smother with brimstone, by blowing the flame and smoke of sulphur into his close cell in Culpeper jail, and who wrote rapturous letters headed,—"From my Palace in Culpeper,"—"a man," says Semple, "of considerable learning, handsome style, affectionate and tender manner, argumentative and eloquent,"—was preaching in the Shenandoah Valley. And so was *John Koontz*, a German, whom enraged persecution often beat and tried to kill, but whom the Lord kept alive till he was eighty years old, and then dismissed to his rest and reward.

Constituted, as we have seen, in 1780, with fourteen members, with the pastoral ministrations of Rev. Joshua Morris, the Church gradually, but slowly, increased in numbers, during the six years that followed. In 1786, Mr. Morris, as we have noticed, removed to Kentucky. How soon after the organization of the Church Mr. Morris became resident Pastor, and how often he preached for them, we have now no means of learning. Whether it was for a while a monthly or semi-monthly station, as from the fewness of its members and their probable inability to support a pastor, seems likely, we have no information.

The first place of meeting, as already noticed, was on Union Hill, at a private house. Afterward a building was erected or procured at or near the North East Corner of Cary and Second streets. Mr. Mordecai, in his interesting reminiscences, writing of Gamble's and Gallows Hill, near where the Penitentiary now stands, says: "One small wooden house, with a shed at either end, stood not far off, in which service was performed by Baptist preachers, for want of a better place of worship. Its locality possessed the advantage of being near the Penitentiary pond—convenient for immersion—for it was then pure water."

Afterward, Dr. P. Turpin presented to the Church the lot on which the First African Church now stands, then on a bluff overlooking the valley and beyond which there was no road, the declivity being too abrupt and steep for vehicles of any sort. Upon this lot a small, plain brick building was erected, which in 1803 and subsequently was enlarged by additions on three sides, making a cruciform edifice one hundred by seventy feet. It was without any pretensions to architectural symmetry, but capable of accommodating a large congregation, and within its walls God displayed his glory and power in the conversion of thousands of sinners, and in the edification of thousands of saints. Some to whom I am now speaking recall tender memories of the Pastors to whom they listened, of precious Christian friends and kin, with whom they were associated in spiritual fellowship, and of the regenerating and pardoning, and adopting grace of God, and of many conflicts in which they were aided, and many gracious experiences which they enjoyed, in connection with the assemblies that gathered in the rude old Church.

After the retirement of the first Pastor, in 1786, Elder John Courtney was called to the pastorate of the Church. He was an humble, plain man, without the advantages of early education, but a godly and laborious minister of Christ, such a one, I fancy, as Chaucer, three hundred years before Courtney was born, aptly described:

> "A true good man there was, of religion,
> Pious and poor, the parson of the town,
> But rich he was in holy thought and work,
> And *thereto* a right learned man, a clerk,
> That Christ's pure gospel would sincerely preach
> And his parishioners devoutly teach."

For several years, Courtney was the only resident Pastor; later, Blair and Rice, of the Presbyterian, and Buchanon and Bishop Moore, of the Episcopal Churches, settled and ministered in the City.

The task of preparing biographical sketches of the Pastors and Ministers connected with the Church has been committed to other hands, and I will not, therefore, attempt any delineation of the character and labors of these worthy men of God. There is a long line of them, and the unity and completeness of this series of services will be best secured by leaving such biographical sketches to the accomplished brother who has, doubtless, given them as careful and thorough study as attainable materials could furnish.

In ten years after its organization, 1790, the number of members had increased to two hundred. From that date we have been able to trace with considerable accuracy the annual statistical returns. The increase has been steady, year by year; no year having passed without some additions by baptism. In 1824, when eighty years of age, Elder Courtney closed his earthly work, and entered upon his heavenly rest. The Church then numbered eight hundred and twenty members. The larger proportion of these were negroes and slaves—"the poor of this world, rich in faith, and heirs of the kingdom."

No charge more unjust was ever made than that the religious instruction and training of the poor and laboring classes was neglected by these early preachers of the gospel. Like their Lord, they could appeal for proof of the divinity of their call by repeating—"the poor have the gospel preached unto them." They were careful, too, in the examination of all applicants for membership, requiring satisfactory testimony of their conversion, and certificates of good character from their employers; and after their admission, they were strict in watchful discipline over their conduct and conversation. Deacons of their own color were appointed to watch over and counsel them, and they listened every Lord's Day to the same instructions and exhortations as their white brethren; and through the zealous teachings of these early preachers and their devoted successors, when the civil war secured freedom to the race, a larger proportion of *them* than of the laboring classes of any other part of the country, or of the world, were professed, regenerate disciples of Jesus Christ.

Associated in pastoral work with Elder Courtney during the closing period of his life—for the Church would not cast him off when advancing years, spent in its service, weakened his physical powers—were *Rev. John Bryce*, for twelve years, from 1810 to 1822; and during one year, 1822, the accomplished and eloquent *Andrew Broaddus;* then for three years, from 1822 to 1825, *Rev. Henry Keeling*. These three were men of much more than average ability. I leave the delineation of their characteristics and services to the abler and more critical pen of Dr. Thomas.

During this period, several other ministers were connected with the Church. *Wm. Braine* was the son of an intelligent and godly mother, who had been a frequent auditor of Whitefield, and a member of the Presbyterian Church, to which the famous Samuel Davies ministered, and afterward a member of Reed's Church, Caroline County. Two of her sons became useful ministers of Christ: *Samuel*, of whom Semple writes: "He was a great preacher, and bade fair to be much greater;" but he died young. *Wm. Braine*, who was a member of this Church, seems to have been an Evangelist, and his work is thus noted in the minutes of Dover Association of 1815: "His labors in the gospel as a minister and servant of the Churches have been more extensive than any other minister in our Association. After a lingering illness, in 1814, he closed his own eyes, clasped his hands, and raised his last prayer: 'Come, Lord Jesus, come quickly,' and without a sigh or groan passed away to a better world."

George Williamson was an occasional preacher, but engaged in secular business, being master armorer in the employ of the State.

Herman Snead, for a time a member of this church, was also enrolled in the list of ministers, and was an early Teacher of youth in this city.

Jacob Gregg was an Englishman, a student in Bristol Academy, and appointed by some British Society Missionary to Sierra Leone on the coast of Africa. After a brief sojourn there, he sailed for America, and landed at Norfolk. After preaching in that vicinity a few years, he traveled into Kentucky and Ohio; but in 1808 or 1809, he returned to Virginia, and settled in Richmond, where he opened and conducted a school for several years. About the year 1817, he was called to the pastoral charge of the New Market Street (now the flourishing Fourth) Baptist Church of Philadelphia. Subsequently he returned to this State. Mr. Gregg was a man of great abilities, and of most amazing memory. It was said of him, that he had committed to memory and could use at will the whole of the Old and New Testaments, and of Watts' Psalms. He had capacity and eloquence enough to place him in the front rank of the preachers of his day. But, unfortunately for his reputation and usefulness, he had acquired an appetite for intoxicating liquors, which he often tried to break with shame and tears, but never, save for intervals, entirely abandoned.

There were no Temperance Societies in his day, and moderate drinking was indulged by all classes. But this miserable habit prevented his filling those high positions for which he had capabilities.

Of *T. Hurst*, whose name is on our list of preachers, I have been able to learn nothing.

Peter Nelson, who for forty years was an honored and successful Teacher in this city, was a graduate of William and Mary College, ordained to the Priesthood in the Episcopal Church, in which he was a minister for twenty years, and after critical investigation he changed his views and church relations, having been baptized by Rev. Andrew Broaddus in 1808 or 1809. He died February 15, 1827, as his physician said, "like a philosopher and a Christian."

Four years before the death of Elder Courtney, viz, in 1820, the Second Baptist Church was organized, seventeen of the members of this Church, with some others, covenanting together in the constitution. There was some friction and alienation connected with this movement— precisely what about we have forgotten if we ever knew. Conscientious Christians will differ about measures and minor doctrines sometimes, but God thwarts the Devil's schemes, and makes them subserve his own ultimate purposes. The Second Church was foreordained of God, has greatly strengthened and widened the influences for good in this community, and has had a most honorable and successful history. *Rev. David Roper*, for a time a member of this Church, who served them as Pastor, while occupied at the same time in responsible clerkships, in the city, lived but seven years in this relation, passing to his eternal rest in 1827. He was succeeded by the faithful, laborious, and ever honored and beloved James B. Taylor, under whose wise ministration the Church steadily grew in power and holy influence.

In 1824, a fresh and vigorous impulse was given to the interests and prosperity of the Church by the induction of *Rev. John Kerr* into the pastoral office. From his distant home Mr. Kerr traveled to Richmond, probably on horseback, or by some still primitive stage coach, for as yet there was no passenger railroad in the world. The great excitement of the year in Richmond was the visit of La Fayette, one of the helpful heroes of the Revolution, a General at twenty years of age, now a veteran of sixty-seven. The old soldiers and their children gathered here from all parts of the State, and the enthusiasm of the reception was wild and exultant.

The contrast between John Courtney and John Kerr was very marked. The one was old and feeble; the other, in the vigor of a healthful manhood, forty-two years old. The one was plain and unassuming; the other, brilliant, eloquent, and aggressive. The one slow, the other rapid, of speech. The one perseveringly plodding; the other, exultantly soaring. The one carrying steadily an oil filled lamp; the other waving a flashing flambeau. The one shining like a quiet star; the other blazing like a refulgent sun. The one opalescent; the other electrical. I suppose few men have ever been given to the pulpit with more genuine native power of attractive and graceful oratory than John Kerr. There have, doubtless, been many, more logical and learned, but few who could so hold, sway and electrify an audience. There have been many who could construct and compose more systematic and finished sermons, but few who could produce such effects upon a congregation. Mr. Kerr's pastorate was the era of increase. During his ministry of eight years, more than twelve hundred converts were baptized and added to the membership of the

Church. There were eight hundred members when John Courtney died, there were sixteen hundred and forty-four in 1832, notwithstanding the secession of *eighty* white members in the Campbellite controversy, which culminated in that year. Mr. Kerr took a decided and prominent part in the discussions which originated in Alexander Campbell's new expositions of gospel doctrines, and which, to a limited extent, divided the Churches in Eastern Virginia, but more widely and disastrously in Kentucky and the West. He was the writer of what are reproachfully branded as "the Dover Decrees," which rendered necessary formal separation from the Reformers, as then called by themselves.

The names of the earliest Deacons and Officers of the Church, and of many of its members, can not now be recalled; but as we trace the existing records, into the first third of the present century, up to the close of Mr. Kerr's pastorate, we find as *Deacons:* Robert Hyde, Anthony R. Thornton, Zachary Lewis, Charles H. Hyde, Onan Ellyson, and Peter Nelson. *Clerks:* H. C. Thompson, Madison Walthall, and Thomas J. Glenn. *Treasurers:* M. Walthall, A. R. Thornton, J. P. Tyler, and Peter Winston, a devout, zealous, and efficient officer of the Church, who died in July, 1841. *Trustees :* David Roper, Robert McKim, and William Dabney.

We also find the names of Joseph Starke, Peter Winston, F. I. Lewis, B. W. Walthall, James Sizer, Richard Reins, Archibald Thomas, James C. Crane, who, in using the office of Deacon well, "purchased to themselves a good degree and great boldness in the faith which is in Christ Jesus;" "also of honorable women who believed and served, not a few." Names not to be forgotten, and for whose godly life and service this church owes thanks to the loving Lord this day, are such as Miss Virginia Ratcliffe, Miss Polly Mauzee, Mrs. Elizabeth Walthall, Mrs. Jane F. Reins, Mrs. R. C. Wortham, Mrs. Peter Winston, Mrs. Winifred Crenshaw, Mrs. Gabriella Bosher, Mrs. M. T. Starke, Miss Emma Williams, Miss Bettie Hillyard, Mrs. Mary E. Hillyard, Mrs. Catharine Thomas, Mrs. Elizabeth Bosher, and a long list of others, who loved the church and served their generation well.

The names, too, of many of the earlier brethren, who, while not in official position, were yet prominent in the counsels of the Church, liberal in its support, and of good repute in the community for integrity and piety, ought to be remembered by us in such a grateful memorial. I can only mention a few who were members of the church previous to 1835. There were such men as S. H. Walthall, William Bosher, Thos. B. Norvell, Royal Parrish, Geo. W. Atkinson, Wm. Tyree, Thomas and Samuel Hardgrove, Richard C. Wortham, Richard Turpin, Stephen Childrey, Jno. L. Turpin, John Watkins, Jas. H. Temple, Wilson B. Hill, Jesse Williams, Spotswood M. Dandridge, and many others of equal worth, though not, perhaps, of equal prominence. Of some of these godly men, interesting and instructive memoirs might be written, had we materials and time.

In comparing the Register of 1835, when the number of white members was three hundred and thirty-three, with the Register of 1880, I find the names of thirteen, who for the forty-five years and more, have lived in fellowship of the church. Three hundred and twenty are gone ; a very few may be still elsewhere living ; all the rest are dead, and most of them, we have good reasons for believing, are with the Lord.

The ministers who were connected with the Church during this period were *Rev. John C. Harrison*, who was for many years Pastor of the Bordentown Church, N. J. He was a brother in good repute, of fair abilities, industrious and wholly given to his work, and quite prominent in the counsels of the denomination.

Barnard Phillips was a very good, plain, uneducated brother, mostly engaged in secular employments, and preaching occasionally.

Jeremiah B. Porter was an earnest, somewhat boisterous preacher, of fair natural abilities, but with little culture.

William Southwood was an Englishman, for a time a student of Cambridge University, and minister of two churches in England before he came to this country. He was an intelligent, conscientious man, well read, a student firm in his convictions, very rigid in his views of church discipline and of Christian character, and with more of force than tenderness in his ministrations. He was six years Pastor in Petersburg, and afterward of St. Stephen's, in King and Queen, where he died in 1850, in the sixty-sixth year of his age.

Joseph Starke, baptized in 1831, served a few years as a Deacon, active and zealous; was dismissed with others to organize the New Bridge Church, and was there called into the ministry, and was an acceptable and honored Pastor of churches in Hanover County.

Jacob Marshall (if I am not mistaken in the man) was a lad who was a member of the same Presbyterian Church with myself in Philadelphia, when we were both boys, he several years the elder. I remember hearing that he had gone South, united with a Baptist Church, and entered the ministry. He was baptized here in 1835. He was a young man of more than ordinary ability, and preached in North Carolina and Georgia. I have often heard favorably of his services, but am not able to trace his career.

Jacob T. Tinsley was temporarily a member of this Church, while a student at the Baptist Seminary, previous to the removal of that institution into the city and its merging into Richmond College.

John O. Turpin still lives, the honored and beloved Pastor of Sharon and Beulah Churches, in King William County. *Robert D. Davenport*, baptized 1831, was a printer, employed in the office of the "Richmond Enquirer," married Miss Mary Frances, daughter of Rev. David Roper, was set apart at the same time as Rev. J. L. Shuck, as Missionary and Superintendent of printing in Siam. He sailed with Mr. Shuck and party in September, 1835. At Bangkok he remained nine years, engaged mainly in printing translations of the Scriptures, both in Siamese and Chinese. He returned in 1845, and died of disease contracted in the East, November 24th, 1849, aged 39 years. He was more useful in his peculiar calling than in the active ministry.

Joseph S. Walthall, baptized in 1831, was a student with Edward Baptist, then of the Baptist Seminary, and afterward graduated at Columbian College, Washington. After his graduation he preached in Columbus, Mississippi, was Tutor in Richmond College, Pastor at Newbern, N. C., and Associate Editor of the "Biblical Recorder," at Raleigh. He returned to Virginia at the breaking out of the war, was in declining health for several years, yet preaching frequently and acceptably, and died in this city, May 20th, 1870. He was an instructive and studious preacher, and an earnest and godly disciple of Christ.

A. Paul Repiton became an able and influential minister of Christ, Pastor for many years in Wilmington, N. C. The closing years of his life were spent in Norfolk and vicinity, where he was Pastor, and where he died in the faith of the Lord Jesus.

Addison Hall was temporarily a member of

this Church. His name and good fame are associated with his efficient work as Pastor in Lancaster and Northumberland Counties.

It is not yet time—and we trust the time is still remote—to sketch the life and services of *Rev. Dr. Ryland,* so long the laborious and conscientious President of Richmond College, and Pastor of the First African Church, and for many years a beloved member of this Church.

Rev. Isaac Taylor Hinton, in 1833, became the successor, after having been for a few months the assistant, of Mr. Kerr. Mr. Hinton had his own peculiar gifts, which admirably fitted in to the needs of the Church at this juncture. He was especially an organizer, constant and untiring in his sacred work, and the great mass of material gathered during the ministry of Mr. Kerr seemed just then to require such talents as he possessed, and as his eloquent predecessor had not possessed. The members were now arranged in six districts, each under the oversight of a Deacon, the blacks with Deacons of their own color. The first register of the Church was prepared and printed; various societies for missionary and benevolent purposes were formed. It was the period of organization. The number of white members, in 1835, was three hundred and thirty-three. About one hundred and sixty were baptized during Mr. Hinton's ministry of two years. During this period the Third—now Grace Street—Church was constituted, with thirty-three members, most of them from the Second Church. *Rev. Henry Keeling* was largely instrumental in gathering these disciples, and in ministering to them while erecting their first humble edifice. During Mr. Hinton's ministry the present site of Richmond College was purchased, and the Virginia Baptist Seminary removed to occupy it. Mr. Hinton was prominent in these aggressive enterprises.

In January, 1836, *Rev. J. B. Jeter* became the Pastor of the Church. It is not for me to speak especially of his character or life. In my judgment—and I have had opportunities for knowing him well, as I was in familiar communication with him for twenty years, and for a time we lived together under the same roof—he was the most perfect Christian gentleman and minister I have ever known. Carlyle says: "If in any sphere of man's life, then in the moral sphere, as the inmost and most vital of all, it is good that there be *wholeness*, and that there be *unconsciousness* which is the evidence of this." Dr. Jeter was a *whole* man, intellectually and morally. His characteristics were symmetrical, rounded, harmonious. There was no development of capabilities and aptitudes in any one direction, at the cost of dwarfing and shrivelling in any other directions. His was not a one-sided, nor a many-sided, but an *all*-sided, intellect and heart. In *any* one direction he had superiors; but taking all his faculties and graces in their aggregate, and there was a completeness and union of character, the like of which is seldom found. And with this was the *unconsciousness* of which Carlyle speaks. Genius is ever a secret to itself. In fact, unity, agreement, is always silent or soft-voiced, it is only discord that loudly proclaims itself. So long as the several elements of Life, all fitly adjusted, can pour forth their movement like harmonious tuned strings, it is a melody and unison. Life from its mysterious fountain flows out, as in celestial music and diapason; like that other music of the spheres, "which never jars harshly upon listening ears." He never exhibited, I do not believe he ever felt, any vain consciousness of his own abilities or attainments. Simple and unasserting as a child; contemplative and thorough as a philosopher. To one other characteristic of

Dr. Jeter, I may be pardoned for alluding. He never became an old man. Seventy eight years had not withered the freshness nor weakened the vigor of his intellectual or spiritual faculties. He kept growing on till he died, and we believe he keeps on growing still. He fell, not as an old oak, whose heart is decayed, and whose sluggish sap can transmit life only to a few stunted leaves; but he fell like a stately palm, in healthful growth, with leafage green and luxuriant, and with wholesome fruit-clusters in bud, and in bloom, and in ripeness, in all successive stages of development.

Now the names of the older Deacons have disappeared from the published Register, only Archibald Thomas, James Sizer, and Richard Reins remaining; while James C. Crane, John Farrar, Christopher Walthall, John Stanard, and Robert H. Bosher occupy the places of the departed. The labors of Dr. Jeter were blessed in the steady increase and edification of the Church. Its members were instructed, encouraged to every good word and work; the moral power and influence of the body over the community, and by benevolent liberality over the State and the world, was augmented.

Dr. Jeter baptized ten hundred and seventy-eight converts into the fellowship of the Church during his pastorate of thirteen and a half years. Gracious and extensive revivals especially blessed five of these years, in each of which over one hundred, and in one of which—1837—two hundred and seventy-two, additions were received. When he entered upon his pastorship there were three hundred and thirty-three white members; when he resigned there were five hundred and sixty-two. During his ministry, from 1836 to 1849, Dr. Jeter became the prominent representative minister of the Baptists of Virginia, in connection with our general work in State and Foreign Missions, in Bible and Publication Societies, in Educational Institutions. The charter for Richmond College was secured and the Institution organized; and the edifice in which we now worship was erected. This building, commenced in 1839, was completed and dedicated October, 1841, at a cost of about $40,000. The erection of this building led to the separation of the white and colored members and the organization of the First African Baptist Church, which continued to occupy the old structure, and which was set apart under the pastoral supervision of Rev. Dr. Ryland, then President of Richmond College. Seventeen hundred and eight colored members remained in the old house, while three hundred and eighty-seven white members removed to the new. During the first year a precious revival, in which the Pastor was aided by Rev. Mr. Robards of New York, added one hundred and sixty-seven by baptism to the Church in its new home. This raised the total, at the close of 1842, to five hundred and thirty-three. There were now four organized churches in Richmond, viz: First, Second, Third,—now Grace Street,—and the First African. In 1846, the Second African Church was constituted under the special superintendence of the Second White Church; and in the same year the Manchester African Church.

The ministers that were members of this Church during the period of Dr. Jeter's ministry who have passed from earth were:

Duncan R. Campbell, D. D. He was born in Perthshire, Scotland, in 1814, and educated at the University of Edinburgh. He entered the Presbyterian ministry, became Pastor of a Presbyterian Church in Scotland, and was for some time an Evangelist in the City of London. He came to this country in 1842, was baptized by Dr. Jeter, and became a member of this

Church. A new body was organized called the Fourth Church, which met in the frame house on Franklin Street, at the corner of Twenty-first Street, where Mr. Campbell preached some six months. He was subsequently Pastor of Mound Bluff and Vernon Churches in Mississippi. The climate being unfavorable to his health, he removed to Kentucky and became Pastor of the Georgetown Church, then Professor of Hebrew and Biblical Interpretation in the Theological Seminary at Covington, and in 1852 was elected President of Georgetown College. This position he held until vacated by his promotion to his higher heavenly sphere. He was a very laborious and zealous minister of Christ, preaching constantly to churches in the vicinity of Covington and Georgetown. His duties in the school did not hinder his filling every Lord's Day with more direct preaching to the people.

The influence of his intellectual and evangelistic labors still blesses the region in which he was best known, and for the ages to come his works will follow him.

Rev. Eli Ball, who removed from New England to Virginia in 1823, and became Pastor of the Church in Lynchburg, came to Richmond about 1826, and became a member of this Church. He was especially an active and zealous agent of our Missionary Boards and of Columbian College. He traveled through all the Southern states, pleading for these evangelizing agencies and successfully forwarding their interests. In 1852, at the request of the Foreign Mission Board, he visited the African colony of Liberia, to survey and suggest measures for the prosecution of our missions there. In his funeral sermon, Dr. Jeter said of him: "Doubtless, Eli Ball will long be remembered by Virginia Baptists as one of their soundest, best, and most useful proclaimers of the glorious gospel." He died in 1853, in the seventy-seventh year of his age.

Rev. Samuel C. Clopton was the first appointed Missionary of the Southern Board to China. He was a student of Columbian College and of the Newton Theological Seminary, and for a time a Tutor in Richmond College. In June, 1846, with the daughter of Rev. Miles Turpin as his wife, he embarked for Canton, China. But he had only time to enter upon preparation for his great work. The Lord called him home on the 7th of July, 1847, in the thirty-second year of his age. He gave bright promise of usefulness in his fervent piety and devout consecration to Christ. But God's ways are wisest. His son, born in China and bearing his name, has taken up the sword of the Spirit that dropped from his dying hand. "Instead of the fathers shall be the children."

William Moncure Gaskins, brother of Mrs. Sarah Jeter, was one of the most promising, talented, and pious of the young ministers of the Church. Hearing him in public prayer, one said: "That man must pray much in secret." He became the Pastor of several churches near Halifax Court House.

Edward Kingsford, D. D., temporarily connected with this Church, and afterward Pastor of Grace Street Church, was a very intelligent and able preacher of the word.

Varay S. Gaskill, baptized in 1846, and licensed afterward, was sent by the Church as a student to Furman Institute, in South Carolina. I have learned nothing of his subsequent career.

Jesse Witt, whose biography is sketched in Dr. Taylor's Virginia Baptist Ministers, was for a time in membership here, probably while agent of our General Association. He was a minister of large influence and usefulness, and died in Texas in 1858.

In 1850, *Rev. Basil Manly, jr.*, succeeded Dr. Jeter in the pastoral office. As he is living still, it is not yet time to enroll his name among those who have finished their course and won their crown. May that time be still remote in the future, that he may accumulate yet richer stores in the service of Christ's churches for the pen of a coming biographer. I may only say that he came to this pastoral charge, shortly after quitting the Princeton Theological Seminary; that by his urbanity, unostentatious piety, devotion to his work, earnest and able expositions and enforcements of divine truth, he won the confidence and the hearts of the people. As President of the Female Institute of this city, he drew a larger number of pupils to its halls than have ever thronged them since, and by whom he is remembered with grateful and loving reverence. As President of Georgetown College, and twice as Professor in our Southern Theological Seminary, he has by his administrative, practical ability and tact, and by his broad and accurate scholarship, contributed much to the efficiency, thoroughness, and prosperity of these institutions. Indefatigable in study and work, amiable and conciliatory in spirit, devoutly interested in every measure that promises good to the kingdom of Christ, he deserves what he has gained, a place in the front rank with the leaders who are most honored, trusted, and loved, in our Southern Israel. During the four years of his pastorate, one hundred and thirty-four were added by baptism to the membership of the Church, and the number increased from five hundred and forty, in 1850, to six hundred and thirty-seven in 1854, when a colony of over one hundred was dismissed, to organize the Leigh Street Church, on Church Hill.

Rev. Reuben Ford—the son of him who bore the same name, and was of illustrious fame among the early champions of religious liberty—was among those thus dismissed, and became the first Pastor of the Leigh Street Church. He was a godly, earnest minister of Christ, and closed his earthly ministry as Pastor in Nashville, Tennessee.

In October, 1854, having been honored with an invitation from the Church, I was received as its Pastor. The number of members, diminished just previous to my coming by the constitution of the Leigh Street Church, was five hundred and eighty-four. For twenty years and three months this relation to you was continued. I have many reasons for profound gratitude and praise to God for the blessings bestowed upon me during this period of my life. I never received from the Church anything but uniform kindness and hearty co-operation in every good work. As far as was possible with so numerous a society, I deemed myself the personal friend of every member, and regarded every member as a personal friend to me. We had no wranglings, no discords, no perturbed or boisterous church meetings. Nothing ever seriously disturbed the peaceful harmony of the Church. The unity and brotherly confidence and regard were as nearly perfect as I have ever known.

The increase of the membership required an enlargement of the board of deacons, and about the year 1858, Dr. Wm. H. Gwathmey was elected and ordained as Deacon, and a few years later brethren A. P. Fox, Wm. G. Dandridge, J. B. Watkins and Geo. J. Sumner, were added to the number.

For a portion of the time we were drawn into closer fellowship with each other by the terrible pressure of the war from without. Our sons and brothers were in daily, deadly peril; and at many a funeral and over many a death where no home burial was possible, we mingled our tears and prayers together. We shared with each other our scant rations, and bore together the fearful privations of a besieged city, and the crushing disappointments and terrible losses and horrors of the closing scenes. I remember well when a brother whose face is now before me came into my study and presented me, as a token of the remembrance and consideration of the brethren from whom he had gathered it, unsolicited and unexpected by me, ten thousand dollars. True it was Confederate money, but it was the only kind you had. Similar evidences of thoughtful kindness, in all conceivable forms I received from many. For twenty years I never had any reason to imagine that I had made a personal enemy in this Church, or in this city outside the Church. And I am sure that no one ever evoked enmity or bitterness from my heart toward him. Pardon me for these allusions, but they are so grateful to me to recall to-day, and I should do violence to my own nature if I did not testify to the Christian magnanimity and delicate consideration,—far beyond my own deservings I know,—with which I was treated by this dear Church through twenty years of service. And

I shall not be accused of vanity if I say that all the powers and capabilities God gave me were constantly and industriously devoted to the service of this Church and to the cause of its Lord and my Lord. Mistakes and errors, oh, yes! there were many; weakness and misjudgments; sometimes impatience and dogmatism; in preaching, often more exacting than tender, sometimes more legal flash than gospel magnet; but with all I can, upon review, honestly say there was an absorbing longing for the growth, efficiency, and spirituality of the Church, and for the conversion of souls to Christ Jesus.

During this period, the Church was twice enlarged, the last time to provide the recess for the choir and organ; the adjoining Infant Class room was built; the Lecture and Sunday School rooms were remodeled, and various alterations and refurnishings were made.

At the beginning of those twenty years, there was peace and large prosperity; then, war and disaster; and at the close, comparative poverty, perplexities, disappointments, and misgivings. It was a period crowded with changes in the world, in our country, in our State, City, Church, in our families, and in ourselves. For me personally it opened with a pleasant home, a loving wife, and little children. It closed upon a homeless, lonely man, with family dead or scattered. In every twenty years are revolutions. Twenty years bear us from Spring time, with its fresh enjoyments and buoyant hopes, through Summer, with its toils and heats, into Autumn, with its matured fruits and falling leaves, toward Winter, with its frosts and fires, its decays and comforts.

Well! Spring has its cheer, Summer its cares, Autumn its chastening, and Winter its consolations. December is not much longer than June. And then, for trustful disciples of Jesus, the merging of Winter into the perennial Spring of God's Paradise!

When I became Pastor, in October, 1854, there were enrolled upon the Register five hundred and seventy-eight members. Of that number only one hundred and ninety-one remained at the close of the twenty years. Three hundred and eighty-seven had gone, through death, removal, or discipline. A considerable number united with the new churches organized during this period, viz. Leigh Street, 1854; Pine Street, 1855; Manchester, 1857. Also, Sidney and Fulton, where this Church sustained out stations and erected buildings, and Venable Street Church.

The Church was blessed with numerous revivals during these twenty years, and with steady healthful increase. The average annual additions were seventy-four. The whole number of additions, fourteen hundred and seventy-nine. Of these, nine hundred and seventeen were converts baptized; four hundred and seventy-seven were introduced upon certificates from other churches; seventy, upon relation of experience; and fifteen were restored upon profession of penitence after exclusion. The whole number of diminutions during the twenty years, by removal, discipline, and death, was eleven hundred and twenty-nine. The net increase, three hundred and fifty; and the total in 1874, eight hundred and ninety.

The roll of the dead for the twenty years contains two hundred and seventy-seven names; enough in numbers, character, piety, and wealth to have formed a strong and effective Church. Of useful ministers united with the Church, we followed to their burial the youthful Z. Jeter, George and Wm. M. Gaskins, and the aged Henry Keeling and Henry W. Watkins. Out of the eight Deacons, who were serving the Church in 1854, five were borne to the cemetery, and their spirits to heaven. The call of their names will awaken a thrill of precious memories in many hearts. Jas. C. Crane, John Farrar, Archibald Thomas, James Sizer, Richard Reins. Taking them altogether, we shall not soon look upon their like again. Two of the clerks of the Church dropped their pens, and read the record of their own enrolment in the unfading book of remembrance: David R. Crane and John H. McCarthy.

Of men in business and professional life, some of whom left a broad mark for good upon their generation and upon the Church, whose lives won respect, and confidence in their religion, and who being dead yet speak, were Richard C. Wortham, James C. Spotts, Royal Parrish, Charles Wortham, Geo. W. Atkinson, James H. Walthall, William Caulfield, John Watkins, John L. Smither, Josiah Dabbs, John Hillyard, Thomas Trowers, Dr. Leon Gelbardt, who gave his life in ministering to yellow fever victims in Norfolk, Dr. Owen B. Hill, Samuel and Thomas Hardgrove, William and Sidney Powers, Wilson B. Hill, Daniel Ward, John L. Ligon, John Turpin, William L. Harrison, Julius A. Hobson, Frederick Butler, Thaddeus B. Starke, Thomas W. Keesee, Samuel Tyack, Thomas Leftwich, Dr. Albert G. Wortham.

Of worthy, pious and promising young men, we may well record in such a historical sketch the names of Alphonzo Dandridge whose funeral was the first I attended in this city—Franklin Caster, John W. Potts, James E. Burnett, James W. Whitlock, and Thomas H. Butler.

Of our young members killed during the war, or who died of wounds or diseases in hospitals and prisons, put upon the record this list: Peyton G. Read, Robert C. Stanard, Henry Cundiffe, John H. Herring, Custis Chamberlayne, George M. Leftwich,—these two last students of Richmond College, and preparing for the ministry,—Washington Tyler, John B. Kate, George W. Smither, Howard K. Cary, Thomas C. Redmond, also a student of the College, William Frayser, Lewis C. Hendricks, Howard S. Wright, John Rogers, Christopher S. Chandler, Thomas S. Hudgens, William J. Wheeler, Columbus A. Daniels, Francis W. Savage, J. T. Iage.

Of aged women, mothers in Israel, and middle-aged women, whose useful lives adorned beautifully their Christian profession, and who, in the home and in the Church, were honored and beloved, what blessed memories and affections will be stirred by the simple mention of their names! An historical sketch could not be complete with their names left out, and some of them deserve permanent biographies, which might be read with more profit and spiritual stimulus than many that have been written. A few of you to-day can recall Charlotte Wooldridge, Patience Pierce, Polly Mauzee, Mary Wortham, Rhoda Thomas, Winnifred Crenshaw, Mary P. Foster, Sarah Durham, Jane Dandridge, Elizabeth H. Greenhow, Susanna Holmes, Nancy Sizer, Isabella Crane, Mary Burton, Mary Lipscombe, Julia A. McCarthy, Mattie Lee Spotts, Harriet Cary, Martha Steane, Fannie W. Leftwich, Elizabeth Dennis, Sarah C. Thompson, Elizabeth Gardner, Mary W. Apperson, Susan R. Childs, Agnes Cowie, Mary J. Rogers, Ann L. Bibb, M. E. M. Gaines, Mildred Turpin, Eleanor Johnson, Susan M. Evans, Ann H. Powel, Sarah Jane Smith, Emeline White, Mary W. Hardgrove, Maria G. Clopton.

Then there was another group of younger women, wives and mothers, who were early called away, some of them from little children to whose care and training they seemed so necessary to mortal eyes. Think of God's precious gifts to the churches of such women, as

Virginia E. Ford, Georgie Bosher, Martha T. Jones, Sarah V. Hooker, Mary C. Wortham, Olivia Bargamin, Frances Lyell, Ella Quesenberry, Lucy Spilman, Mary W. Williams, Margaret L. Patterson, Jane L. Anderson, Carrie V. Ryland, Agnes W. Terrell, Edmonia Slaughter, Mary T. Harris, Elizabeth & Louisa Dandridge, Ella J. Lipscombe and Virginia B. Smith.

We can scarcely conceive of a purer, nobler band of Christian women than these, for usefulness on earth and for blessedness in heaven.

There was another group of unmarried women, some of them were girls, whom the Lord prepared by early conversion for early transfer to heaven, as Betty Clopton, Martha Braxton, Adaline Meredith, Mattie Lee Hudgens, Eliza Gannaway, Eliza and Nannie Meredith, Susan and Margaret Farrar, Virginia Burke, Pamelia Ford, Laura Alvey, Ada B. Winfree.

This is no mere dull catalogue of names, as it may sound to some. They represent those who belong to the history of the Church, and through whose influence that history has been made. Our dead of an hundred years—a great cloud of witnesses—we may imagine as in the sanctuary to-day, looking out through shadowy veils, imperceptible to mortal vision. Upon seats they once filled, and faces they once loved, and results their prayers and piety helped to attain. How can we tell what ranges disembodied spirits may take? However, all this may be, there is a sense in which we listen to the voices of the dead. Influences do not die and memories of the pious dead are still means of grace to the struggling living. "They rest from their labors and their works do follow them."

Of those still living who were connected with the Church between 1833 and 1874, is a noble band of faithful and effective Christian ministers, whose biographies will be written when their work on earth is finished, and many of whom are winning fame and love among our Churches. We may simply record the names of John O. Turpin of King William County; James G. Council of Mathews County; Dr. Joseph R. Garlick, Alexander H. Sands, Francis C. Johnson of Georgia; Dr. Poindexter S. Henson of Philadelphia; Dr. W. D. Thomas of Norfolk; W. Harrison Williams of Charlottesville; William S. Ryland of Kentucky; Dr. M. Bryan Wharton of Georgia; Isaiah T. Wallace of Henrico; Lansing Burrows of Lexington, Kentucky; Richard W. Norton of Tennessee; Dr. A. W.

Read of Orange; William H. Tucker, M. D., of Louisiana; A. A. Lomax of Mississippi; John Blenner, first Pastor of the German Church in this city; James L. Vass of South Carolina; Julian M. Luck, Edmund Harrison, John Hart, J. L. M. Curry, H. A. Tupper, crowning the climax.

From this long and honorable list I have omitted the names of three, who from various causes, have left the ministry of our denomination. Only three of the large number have failed to illustrate and confirm the wisdom of the Church in authorizing them to preach the gospel of Christ.

To this list I have yet to add the names of six of our honored ministers, who died during my pastorate, and at whose funeral services I was called to officiate. Of three of these I have already spoken, viz: *Joseph S. Walthall, Henry Keeling, and William M. Gaskins. Z. Jeter George*, graduated at Richmond College in 1853. He was a student for a time at the University of Virginia, preaching on Sundays in the neighboring county churches. In 1857, he became the first Pastor of the Manchester Church. He died in 1858, in the twenty-seventh year of his age. He was a brother of lovely spirit, earnest piety, and gave bright promise of usefulness.

Henry Watkins had passed his three-score and ten, and had for many years been preaching the gospel of Christ, with little worldly compensation. His life was a beautiful illustration of the meekness, patience, and charity which the gospel he studied and loved develops. He was Pastor of churches in Powhatan and Chesterfield, and preached steadily for some years to the Belvidere, now Pine Street, Church. He passed to his blessed home in March, 1872.

George William Keesee was born in 1831, baptized in the sixteenth year of his age. Graduated from Richmond College in 1851, spent two years at the University of Virginia, was Pastor first of Hicksford Church, and then of Goldsboro Church in North Carolina, where he died in 1861, in the thirtieth year of his life. He was amiable in natural disposition, and this temper was sweetened by divine grace. Of his college course, Dr. Ryland said, he could not recall a single irregularity that deserved reproof from his teacher. As a preacher he was studious, careful, and conscientious in preparation, clear and earnest in delivery. By his piety and his gentle and affable bearing he won the confidence and love of his people, and his memory is still tenderly cherished by them and by all who knew him.

A brief *resumé*, comparing the condition of the Church in 1780 and 1880, may be a fitting close to this discourse. A population of 1800, in 1780, has grown to some sixty-five thousand in 1880. One Baptist Church of fourteen members, in 1780, has swelled into nineteen—including Manchester, into twenty-one—Churches in 1880; more than one Church for every individual member. Those fourteen members have increased more than a thousand fold in a century, numbering in 1880, 16,847 members, including Manchester. In 1780, there was one Baptist member to every 128 of the whole population; in 1880, about one to every four of the whole population. Taking all Christian evangelical denominations, leaving out Roman Catholics and Jews, instead of two feeble Churches in 1780, we have fifty Churches with 25,000 members, and instead of one, we have fifty houses of worship, the smallest of which is probably larger than St. John's was then.

In fifty years—from 1824 to 1874—there were thirty-five hundred and thirty-eight persons, professing conversion, baptized into the fellowship of this single Church, an average of over seventy a year. Probably a number equal to half of that united by certificate or letter, making some fifty-three hundred who had united with the Church during the half century. Yet, in 1874, there were only twenty-four persons who had been members in 1835. In January, 1880, there were only fifteen who were members of the Church in 1835, and two of them—Mrs. Elizabeth Bosher and Mrs. Catharine Thomas—two of Christ's saints—have since passed away.

Of the five and a half years that have passed since 1874, it is not my place particularly to speak. I need only say that the steady, prudent, judicious, untiring, and consecrated services of Rev. Dr. E. W. Warren have been blessed of God to the maintenance and enlargement of the efficiency and intelligence of the Church; and that the fervid eloquence, and zeal, and devotion of your present pastor, Rev. Dr. J. B. Hawthorne—perhaps the most like to John Kerr, in the long line of pastors—gives promise of still more rapid increase and efficiency, than during any period of the past. May God grant that these buds of promise may ripen into abundant clusters of wholesome fruits as year after year rolls by.

SKETCHES OF DECEASED PASTORS.

BY W. D. THOMAS.

DECEASED PASTORS.

IN reviewing the history of this Church, which, under God, has been the source of so many holy, widely-diffused, and potent influences, it is eminently appropriate that special mention should be made of those who have presided over it as Pastors and Bishops, and who have already fallen on sleep. But in assigning places, at this Centenary Celebration, for the particular mention of its Pastors and Officers, the Church does not mean to intimate that such only have been agents in the upbuilding of Zion. During all these hundred years of church life, holy men and women, occupying no prominent positions, holding no office, have by their prayers, by their godly living and diligent activities, contributed largely to its progress and efficiency. It would be a joy on this occasion to make honorable mention of such humble and useful servants of our God; but it cannot be. Many of them are forgotten; even their names are unknown to us. They have lived, labored, died, and in so short a time have been forgotten upon the earth. It is a sad reflection to us; but it does not trouble them. They are rejoicing, because their names were inscribed upon the imperishable roll of heaven, written in the Lamb's Book of Life. And as to their work, that abides ever upon the earth. It may be hidden out of our sight; but it none the less has its place, and is represented in the Church of to-day. The influence of these forgotten followers of our Lord has survived their names. By ways we know not, along paths we cannot trace, that influence has reached us, has infused itself into our life, has helped to make us. And while gratefully cherishing the memory of those who have been over us in the Lord, we also from our hearts to-day give thanks to God for the nameless and forgotten saints into whose labors we have entered.

The first Pastor of this Church was Rev. Joshua Morris. He was born in James City County; but the exact date of his birth is not known. The Church Manual of 1875 places his death in the year 1838, and at the age of seventy-seven years. If this be so, then he was only nineteen years old when he came to Richmond, and was already preaching in the sixteenth year of his age. Dr. Spencer, of Kentucky, says, he died in 1837, and was largely over eighty years old. This statement, we judge, is nearer the fact, since it is not probable that he began preaching at so early an age as fifteen or sixteen years. Nothing is known of his family beyond the fact, mentioned in Semple's history, that "his father and uncle preached occasionally." He began his Christian life as a member of the James City Church. Whether he was baptized by Elisha Baker, the founder, or by John Goodall, the first Pastor of that Church, we cannot say. He was preaching in the year 1775 or 1776.

Mr. Semple tells us, that Elder Baker began his labors in Grafton in 1775, that "in no great while several were baptized, and Joshua Morris, a young preacher of considerable gifts, from James City, watered the plants." We next trace him as residing in the bounds, and laboring in connection with the Boar Swamp Church—now Antioch. We do not know when he entered upon his ministry there; but while serving that Church he began also to preach in Richmond at the house of a Mr. Franklin.

His labors were not fruitless. Some few were baptized, and he himself removing to Richmond, a Church was established under his care in 1780. Thus the little town, which had been only a preaching station of a somewhat flourishing country Church, rose to the dignity of having its own Church and resident Pastor. It was a feeble body of only fourteen members. Elder Morris continued to be its Pastor for six years.

We have now no records from which to judge of his preaching here or trace the progress made under his ministry. The fact that the little band, worshipping at first in a private house, soon erected a small frame "meeting-house," indicates some advance, and shows at least some energy and something of a progressive spirit both in the Pastor and the Church.

The few brief notices of this servant of the Church make the impression that he was a minister of earnest spirit, readily embracing and diligently seeking opportunities of useful labor. He may have been without education, and there is no reason to believe that he was a brilliant preacher, since the discriminating and cautious Semple describes him as having "considerable gifts." He removed from this city to Kentucky in the year 1786. The impressions made by the few notices of his ministry and labors in this State are deepened and elevated by his busy and useful career in Kentucky. Into this field I am enabled to follow him by the kindness and diligence of Dr. Burrows and of Dr. Spencer, who is now engaged in collecting materials for a history of the Baptists of Kentucky. Elder Morris was introduced to a Church in Jefferson, now Shelby, County, Kentucky, by William Hickman. In speaking of one of his journeys into Shelby County, then on the frontiers of civilization, to preach for some of the settlers in the forts, Mr. Hickman says: "We crossed the river one at a time, and swam our horses by the side of the canal. We had then twenty miles to go in the night. Sometimes it was snowing and then the moon shining. We crossed Benson nineteen times. At some fords the ice would bear us over, at other fords some steps would bear us and then we would break in. We passed a number of evacuated cabins, the owners of which had been killed or driven off by the Indians. About two o'clock in the morning we knocked at the fort-gate for admittance. The old gentleman was not at home and the old lady had all barred up. It was some time before we could convince her who we were, as she was afraid of a decoy. But at last she let us in."

There was a Church of eight members at this place, called Brashear's Creek. Mr. Hickman was urged to settle among them, but could not. They asked him to recommend a preacher to them. He says: "Brother Joshua Morris had just moved to the county, and I thought he would suit them. I saw him, told him the situation of the people and their wish. I told him, if he would like a tour there, I would go with him. We both went. Soon after, he moved, and his labors were much blessed, and many a tour I took with him afterwards long circuits around."

This Church, since merged into the Shelbyville Church, was at Bracket Owen's Fort, near the present site of Shelbyville. It was constructed in 1785, by William Taylor and John Whitaker, on the very frontiers of civilization in that direction. Assaults by the Indians were frequent, and the farmers ploughed under arms.

In subsequent visits Mr. Hickman and his associates would be met at the Kentucky River by an escort of friends. Sometimes twenty or more armed brethren marched with the preachers as they went from station to station to preach the gospel. At this outpost the first Pastor settled with his family.

About ten miles north of Owen's Fort, on Fox Run, was another fort and settlement. Here Elder Morris preached occasionally, and on January 26, 1794, gathered the Christian immigrants and baptized converts, and, aided by Elder John Whitaker, organized the Fox Run Church of fifteen members. It is now a flourishing Church in the town of Eminence, and retains its original name. William Marshall, uncle of the Chief-Justice, became its first Pastor. On Elk Creek, twelve miles south of Owen's Fort, was another preaching station. Here on April 27, 1794, Elder Morris constituted the Elk Creek Church, of ten members. It has become one of the famous churches of Kentucky. Dr. Spencer thinks it highly probable that he was also "the chief instrument in gathering the Buck Creek and Long Run Churches in the same region, and which have ever since been influential and useful churches. Toward the close of the century Elder Morris moved northward, into what is now Carroll

County, and gathered the Ghent Church. In 1800, April 5, in connection with William Hickman and others, he organized the Port William Church, Carroll County, of which he became a member and Pastor, and which in later years became united with the Ghent Church. From Carroll County he moved to Nelson County and became the successor of Elder Joseph Barnett (formerly of Virginia) as Pastor of the Cedar Creek Church, next to the oldest Church in Kentucky. This was his home the remainder of his life. He was also Pastor of Mill Creek Church, in the same county, and for eighteen months (1801–2) supplied the pulpit of the Severns Valley Church, now Elizabethtown. In this time he received into that Church one hundred and forty-six members, most of whom he baptized. Among them were Isaac Hodgen, who became one of the most brilliant and useful ministers of the State, and several others who also became preachers.

In 1816, assisted by Jeremiah Vardeman and George Waller, a glorious revival blessed his Mill Creek Church. In 1819, in connection with Moses Pierson and Isaac Taylor, he aided in constituting New Hope Church, in Washington County, ever since an efficient country Church.

Dr. Spencer says of him: "In person, Mr. Morris was rather below medium height, of stout build, with a tendency to corpulency." In later years, he became so unwieldy from this tendency as not to be able to go far from home. He was scrupulously neat in his dress and elegantly dignified in bearing. As a preacher, he was hardly up to mediocrity. He spoke rapidly, with great energy and boldness. "He spoke as one having authority, reproved every species of immorality and sin with uncompromising faithfulness and plainness. He was a man of practical wisdom. As far as known, every church which he gathered, and every one with which he was connected (except Brashear's Creek, which was wisely merged into the Shelbyville), are still in existence, and several of them strong and influential churches."

Surely the memory of this grand old pioneer missionary and planter of our ever-green churches deserves to be cherished by the child of his youth.

Rev. John Courtney, the Second Pastor of this Church, was born in King and Queen County, in the year 1744, and was reared under Episcopal influences, his father and eldest brother being, we are told, "conspicuous and influential members of that church." He lacked the advantages of education. Being quite young when his father died, and the estate passing legally to the eldest son, he was, it is said, "bound apprentice to the business of a carpenter." Beyond this nothing is known of his early years. He is represented as being naturally of a generous, frank, and independent spirit. The date of his conversion cannot be fixed with precision. He was probably baptized by Rev. John Young, by whom the Upper College Church—now Rehoboth, in King William County—was planted, and of which Elder Courtney became the first Pastor. Mr. Semple tells us that this Church "prospered under his care." He is said to have taken an active part in the revolutionary struggle. Dr. Jeter expressed the opinion that had he been exempt from military duty, as under the Colonial Laws he was not, it is probable his patriotism would have taken him to the field. In support of his opinion, he tells us that when more than seventy years of age, in response to a call for volunteers made by the Governor of the State under apprehension of an invasion of the city by British troops, Elder Courtney appeared on the Public Square, musket in hand. He adds:

"The moral influence of such a spectacle must have been thrilling."

From his first field of labor, Mr. Courtney removed to Richmond and entered upon his pastorate here in the year 1788. He was already in the forty-fifth year of his age, and until his death, thirty-six years later, served the Church either as its exclusive or Senior Pastor. His labors were greatly blessed. During his pastorate the Church erected a new house of worship, and some years before his death had occasion to enlarge it.

Mr. Semple, writing of Richmond in 1809, says: "Here, although the Baptists are not the most flourishing sect, they stand upon respectable ground; they have built, by public subscription, a large brick meeting-house, and probably move on, both as respects discipline and the conducting of public worship, with as much regularity as any people in the Union"—viz., the First Union Meeting District, in Dover Association. "Their Pastor, Elder Courtney, took the care in the year 1788, and under his labors they have enjoyed peace and prosperity." According to the ideas then prevalent amongst our people and preachers, he received no stipulated salary. At the close of the morning service on Lord's Day, a hat collection was taken by Deacons at each door of the Church. The money thus collected was emptied into the handkerchief of the senior Deacon, wrapped up, carried to the Pastor's house, and put into a bowl in the cupboard. This same, much or little, was his salary. The sisters of the Church, by presents, from time to time, kept him in clothing. The further needs of his family were supplied by the labor of his own hands.

He was a man without culture, but of vigorous mind. As a preacher, he possessed no brill'ant gifts; was plain, earnest, very little, if any, above the average of the Baptist preachers of his day. He occupied a high position in the Dover Association, and sometimes presided over that body. His preaching was doctrinal and intensely Calvinistic. As remembered in his latter years, he was corpulent, with long white hair, and venerable in appearance. His voice was musical. The first Mrs. Robert Ryland attributed her religious awakening to the impression made by hearing Father Courtney repeat, in musical, tremulous, and solemn tones, the hymn beginning "That awful day will surely come."

It is said that he lacked breadth of view, was

unprogressive; that his religious views and plans of effort were stereotyped at the close of the Revolutionary War, and that, in his opinion, all subsequent changes were portentous of deterioration and ruin. He opposed Sunday Schools as a desecration of the Sabbath; the use of hymn books, in public worship, except by the preacher, because the churches had no such custom. One exception, however, to his usual opposition to things new is worthy of special notice. When female prayer-meetings first began, they excited much opposition, and appeal was made to old Father Courtney for his opinion. Mrs. Halsey—mother of the more widely known Mrs. John Hollins—often told how he replied that "he had never heard of praying doing anybody any harm; and for his part the sisters might pray on." On the other hand, his tenacity for things old finds a characteristic illustration in the following fact. Some of his young people were ambitious that their venerable Pastor should be more up to the times. On one occasion a young lady ventured to suggest that his pronunciation was not altogether correct, and, as an example, told him that he said "*moloncolly*." Upon his asking, "What ought I to say, honey?" she answered "*melan-*

choly." The good old man replied, "I like *moloncolly* the best." His unprogressiveness was due rather to his lack of early advantages of education than to his heart. He was neither dictatorial nor obstinate. Kind and forbearing in spirit, he learned to acquiesce in measures introduced against his will.

As a Pastor, he was discreet, diligent, and sympathetic. Even when too old and infirm to dismount from his horse he rode, cane in hand, from door to door, and calling the friends out to him would encourage, counsel, and exhort them, sometimes closing his interview with prayer on horseback in the street. His manly character, godly sincerity, consistent and devout life, commanded universal respect. He was free from worldly ambition. In his dress, his manners, his style of preaching, and mode of life, it was most obvious that he did not seek admiration. He was much in the habit of quoting in his sermons the couplet:

> "No foot of land do I possess,
> Nor cottage in this wilderness."

Some one at last gave him—not, perhaps, actually transferring by deed, but virtually a gift—a house and lot. Soon after, in preaching, he began to quote his favorite couplet, but stopped in the midst and corrected himself. Afterwards he saw his generous friend and returned the property, saying, he would rather have his lines than the house. Father Courtney's success was due far more to his eminent piety, sound judgment in pastoral work, and the exercise of wholesome discipline, than to the attractiveness and ability of his preaching.

At the time of his death the Church numbered about a thousand members, more than two-thirds of whom probably were colored people. No Pastor ever enjoyed in higher measure the confidence and affection of his people. The strongest testimony to which is the fact that when the increasing infirmities of age prevented him from fully meeting the demands of the field, the Church procured an Assistant Pastor, and continued the plan for thirteen or fourteen years. He died December 18th, 1824, an old man, full of years, and meet for heaven. It cannot be doubted that chiefly to the influence and labors of Father Courtney must be attributed that conservative religious spirit which has distinguished this Church through all its history.

Rev. John Bryce began his labors as the assistant of Father Courtney about 1810, and continued them, with an interruption of a few months, for about twelve years. It is believed that he was born in Goochland County; this, however, is not definitely known. He was educated for the legal profession, but left the law for the pulpit. He was of commanding appearance, and his hair retained its glossy blackness until his death at the age of seventy-six years. He was a man of undoubted talent, a superior preacher, and quite an orator. The Senior Pastor entertained for him, and always manifested towards him, a fatherly affection. The warm-hearted, affectionate Assistant returned the affection with filial spirit. There was between them no rivalry, no jealousy. From 1823-26 Mr. Bryce resided in Fredericksburg, where he preached and practised law. Mr. Semple remonstrated with him, urging that this course would injure his usefulness and influence with his brethren. Mr. Bryce replied, that the course was necessary for the support of his family. He was never careful about his finances, and Mr. Semple said, that if he had received a thousand dollars, he would certainly spend fifteen hundred; and even if he received fifteen hundred he would as certainly spend two thousand.

He afterwards removed to Kentucky, and engaged in the practice of law. Unfavorable reports as to the consistency of his life became prevalent. But he afterwards resumed the work of the ministry, and closed a useful life at Henderson, Kentucky, in the year 1864, at the ripe age of seventy-six.

Rev. Andrew Broaddus, of Caroline County, was the Associate of Father Courtney during the interval of about nine months mentioned above. He was the Apollos of the Virginia pulpit, and his praise is to-day in all the churches. His published memoir renders unnecessary, even if the short time of his connection with this Church warranted, a sketch of his useful career.

In 1822, Rev. Henry Keeling became Co-pastor of the Church, and after the death of Elder Courtney was really, if not nominally, its Pastor for about twelve months. He was the son of Rev. Henry Keeling, Sr., a native of Princess Ann County, who at the age of eighteen became a member of the Church in Norfolk. Mr. Keeling was one of the early pupils in the class or school then taught in Philadelphia by Drs. William Staughton and Irah Chase, which afterwards grew into Columbian College. His usefulness in what is now called distinctively pastoral work was hindered by his lack of a genial and social nature. He prepared his sermons with great care. His preaching was highly intellectual, without pathos, without warmth, and, in fact, "cold as frost." He resigned about the year 1825, and became the head of a flourishing School for young ladies. He was also the Editor of the "*Religious Inquirer;*" and became yet more widely known as the Editor of "*The Baptist Preacher.*" In the latter years of his life he became the subject of damaging suspicion, which caused great pain and perplexity to his brethren. He died in 1870, at the age of seventy-six.

Rev. John Kerr entered upon his Richmond pastorate in March, 1825. He was born in Caswell County, North Carolina, in 1782. His father was of Scotch descent, a Baptist, and said to have been eminently pious. His mother, a sister of Gen. Azariah Graves, was a lady of the highest social position. She was distinguished for great excellence and energy of character, and as a mother was careful and wise in the rearing of her children. His early education, though not thorough and liberal, was superior to that of most of those about him. His boyhood was spent in near proximity to excellent schools, his parents were such as might be expected to appreciate the importance of education, and doubtless furnished him the best opportunities they could afford. His younger brothers are known to have been well educated. In early boyhood, it is said, he acquired readily, and that his disposition and manners made him quite a favorite. He had both in boyhood and manhood the advantage of association with the intelligent and cultured.

He was converted while teaching in the family of a relative. He attended, out of curiosity and for sport, a meeting then in progress at a Presbyterian Church, and was stricken down by the power of the truth and of the Holy Spirit. His conversion was attended with pungent conviction and great joy. The date of his conversion cannot be fixed, but he was baptized, it is said, August 12th, 1801, when nineteen years old. He delivered a discourse on the day of his baptism. Soon afterwards he entered the ministry, and was ordained in his native county. Then he travelled extensively in his own State and in the States of South Carolina, Georgia, and Virginia, coming in contact and association with the more distinguished ministers of the time. In 1805, he was married to Mrs. Elizabeth Williams, and settled in Halifax County, where he preached, charming all by his eloquence, and we cannot doubt turning many to righteousness.

In 1810 or 1811, he became a candidate for Congress and was defeated. He was afterward elected, and was in Congress from 1812–1816. His entrance into political life was not regarded with favor by his brethren, and exerted, as he afterwards said, an injurious spiritual influence upon himself. At one time he had almost, if not quite, decided to give himself wholly to the practice of law. A fall from his horse, by which his leg was fractured and his life imperilled, became the occasion of most serious reflection, and he afterwards gave himself with fresh consecration to the ministry. He continued to preach in Halifax County until 1825, but it is not possible now to record the result of his labors. Crowds attended upon his ministry, and as a preacher he was almost idolized by the people. In March, 1825, he became Pastor of this Church, and served it for eight years. His ministry here was generally successful. Nine hundred and fifty-seven converts were baptized into the Church, and the social character of its membership was greatly elevated. All the enterprises of the denomination received the benefit of his sympathy and his magnetic fervor.

This success was not due to his pastoral work, for in this direction he was not industrious nor active, although of genial nature and in social intercourse attractive; nor was it in any degree due to his administrative and organizing ability, for in these respects he seems to have been utterly deficient. His success was emphatically that of the *preacher*. He had all the advantages belonging to an imposing personal appearance, to a sonorous and melodious voice, to ease, grace, and dignity of manner, and to fluency of speech. His mind moved quickly; his feelings were ardent and intense; his imagination was royal; his powers of description rarely, if ever, surpassed; and his diction often majestic. Defects of method, of exegesis, of matter, and often of taste, were all forgotten under the spell of the pathos and eloquence by which he moved the hearts of men. Crowds flocked to hear him whenever he preached. All ages, all classes felt and confessed the power of the orator. He did not write his sermons, but I am able, through the kindness of Rev. E. Dodson, of North Carolina, to quote from a sermon delivered by Mr. Kerr in North

Carolina, in 1828, at the funeral of Colonel Joseph Williams. It may help to form some idea of the eminent preacher, although we lack the preparation into which he had brought his hearers, and must miss the electric power of the speaker. Referring to the manner of the Judgment, Mr. Kerr said:

"We have heard of well trained armies meeting in deadly conflict with banners waving high. We have heard the warrior's shout, the cannon's roar, the clash of arms and clangor of trumpets, mingling with the shrieks and groans of dying thousands. But what are all these compared with the second appearance of him who once visited this world in the form of a servant, and became obedient unto death. Behold his great white throne. Behold, he cometh with clouds, with the voice of the archangel and the trump of God, with ten thousand of his saints and with all his glory, —with the glory of the Father and the holy angels,—with the thunders and fires of heaven's artillery playing and flashing around him,—with myriads of winged reapers brandishing flaming sickles, ready to reap the great harvest of the earth. Behold his face, once bathed in sweat and tears and blood, now shining with such lustre that the sun blushes into everlasting night, and the moon bleeds, and the heavens and the earth start from their long established position and flee away, and there is found no place for them.

"We have heard of earthquakes shaking the globe and filling the world with consternation ; of volcanic mountains belching out their burning lava and desolating the surrounding regions, —but what are all these compared with the last groans of an agonizing and expiring universe,— with the awful grandeur of that moment when the retiring earth shall pause in her flight, obedient to the voice of him who has the keys of death, and opening her bosom surrender her myriads of long held captives? Now we behold the dead, small and great, stand before God. Now we behold Adam and his last son with their intermediate connexions in order before the face of him who sits upon the throne. Here Judas Iscariot and Pilate and Caiaphas shall see him upon the throne, whom they betrayed and condemned. Here Herod and John the Baptist, and Paul and Felix, shall have their last interview. Here the blood-stained tyrant shall meet the victims of his power ; the midnight assassin, covered with gore, shall face him who fell beneath his dagger; the unfeeling votary of Mammon shall stand before the widow and orphan who groaned under his iron hand. O my soul, how great the day, how grand, how awful the exhibition!"

Many incidents have been told indicating his power over masses, and over persons of every rank in society and every degree of cultivation. Sometimes, in those days of fearless freedom, some would fairly shout under his preaching. Mr. Kerr had his own way of controlling and regulating such demonstrations. On one occasion an old shouting sister exclaimed, "I want to go home to heaven and stay in this wicked world no longer." Mr. Kerr said to her "Wait, my sister; don't start on foot; wait till your Heavenly Father shall send his chariot and steeds of light." In 1832, Mr. Kerr resigned his pastorate, in order to devote himself to the work of an evangelist, but was induced to continue nominally the Pastor of the Church, until towards the close of 1833. Historical fidelity requires me to add, that by this time his lack of close application and studious habits was beginning to tell upon his ministry here, despite his splendid gifts as an orator.

After his removal from Richmond, he settled

near Danville, and spent the remainder of his life chiefly in evangelistic labors, crowds always attending his preaching, and multitudes converted under it. He died on the 29th day of September, 1842. It is gratifying to know that, after long neglect, a monument has been recently erected to mark the grave of this great and good man.

Rev. Isaac Taylor Hinton, the successor of Mr. Kerr, was a native of the city of Oxford, England. His father was a man of culture and Pastor of the Baptist Church in Oxford. His mother was a sister of the celebrated Isaac Taylor. Two of his brothers were Baptist ministers. Mr. Hinton was well educated, chiefly by his father. In early life he was engaged in the printing business. In 1830, he came to this country and resided for two years in Philadelphia.

In April, 1833, he was invited to Richmond as an Assistant to Mr. Kerr, and on the 29th of December of the same year was unanimously elected sole Pastor. He was a very superior preacher; acute, able, and instructive. This was his first pastoral charge, and he gave himself to his work with zeal and constant industry. The Church steadily increased and improved under his care. He was a man of great system, of remarkable ability as an organizer. In 1835, Mr. Hinton resigned his charge, moved first to Chicago, then to St. Louis, and in 1844 to New Orleans. Here he fell a victim to the yellow fever in August, 1847, while lovingly and actively ministering to the sick and dying.

Rev. Dr. J. B. Jeter, just gone to heaven, was born on the 18th day of July, 1802, in the county of Bedford, that nursing mother of so many distinguished ministers of the gospel. He became the Pastor of this Church on the first Lord's Day of the year 1836, and was its faithful and efficient servant for more than thirteen years. During this time he baptized nearly a thousand converts, and the Church made steady and healthful progress. It was under his pastorate that this house of worship was erected, and the colored membership was organized into a separate Church.

It is impossible to estimate the extent to which the Church is indebted to these wise steps for its development and progress. The "Recollections of a Long Life," so recently written by himself, the admirable biographical sketch published immediately after his death, and the complete biography soon to be issued, render any detailed account of his career and services unnecessary here and now. We know that not only this Church, but all our churches, and all the enterprises of our denomination have felt the mighty influence of his counsels, his efforts, and his spirit. We know that, of all the Virginia Baptist preachers, he was the most influential in his own State, and the most widely known beyond it.

It would be a mournful pleasure to speak at length of such a man, whom it has been my privilege to reverence from my youth up, and by whose ministry my early spiritual life was nourished. Even if time allowed it, the much which has been said and written, and which need not be repeated here, would exclude me from such a privilege. And yet your patience will indulge me just a little to speak of him.

He was not when he assumed this pastorate, nor when he resigned it, just the man he was when he died. For he belonged to that order of men, "elect and precious," who keep on growing through a long life, and who attain the very flower of their manhood at the age when others enter their second childhood.

He was an example of the influence of Christianity upon intellectual as well as moral development. It is true that he was well endowed by nature. He did not receive the imperial gift of genius; nor do I claim for him the capacity of profound thought; nor yet of extraordinary logical powers; but he undoubtedly possessed by nature unusual mental vigor and clearness of vision, while thirst for knowledge and the desire to excel characterized him from childhood. In his case, as in that of every regenerate man, his natural endowments constituted the raw material out of which the spiritual man was made. But such natural gifts as his, under the sway of mere natural ambition, would never have made the Dr. Jeter, whom we know, intellectually any more than morally. The influence of his personal experience of God's grace; the influence of the resolutions, the hopes, and the responsibilities of the gospel firmly believed—this it was which quickened all his powers, nerved and braced his will, directed his aspirations, helped to make constant and untiring his application, and so actually developed his potentialities, and made the man.

I cannot venture to speak of his spiritual manhood; time fails us. I mention only one or two rare combinations in his character.

He was a man of strong convictions, and

tenacious of his opinions. He would, I know, readily enough yield when *convinced* of error, but it was *not easy* to convince him. He was also as much bent, as any man, upon making his convictions the convictions of others also. Yet he possessed such sublime generosity of forbearance, as to make it impossible for him to be bitter or even discourteous towards others, not agreeing with him. Blessed combination of splendid qualities!

He was—at least as I saw him—fully conscious of his own powers. This is true of every man who is born to lead. Yet he was truly humble. Free from vanity, he was equally free from an assumed and pretentious humility. They were equally alien to his realness. But I cannot portray him. He was as Dr. J. A. Broadus has well said, "Saul in stature and Samuel in spirit." But you know him, and for the privilege, many of you will thank God on earth and in heaven. Oh, even as John the Baptist came in the power and spirit of Elijah, so may God also send us others in the power and spirit of Jeremiah Bell Jeter "of blessed memory."

After the resignation of Dr. Jeter, the Church remained without a Pastor for some time. The pulpit was supplied occasionally by the late Dr. James B. Taylor, and the Rev. Dr. Robert Ryland, still spared to the world, and whom we welcome here to-day; and for several months by the Rev. C. B. Jennett, young, handsome, gifted, and pious, who died in Augusta, Georgia, at the early age of twenty-seven years.

Ye are God's building, and these are the laborers, whom, having finished their appointed work upon his house, he has taken into rest. They were very unlike each other; but they were all yours, and the same Lord gave them. He wisely sent them one after another to do the needed work. With their different gifts they have wrought at different stages in the progress of the building—some digging out the foundation; some laying down the lowest stones, soon all covered up and out of sight; some bringing together the lively stones; some arranging and placing them in position; some cementing and riveting them together; and some, with delicate skill, polishing and adorning. The workmen are many and the workmanship is varied, but the building is one; and all the work wrought upon it in the name of the Lord shall abide forever. So that in the end, the building finished, the builders shall all rejoice together, and that old strife, "Who shall be accounted the greatest," together with that old division, "I am of Paul, and I of Apollos, and I of Cephas," over forever, shall with one mind and one heart join in the song, "Not unto us, but unto thy name be the glory."

HOUSES OF WORSHIP.

BY

W. H. GWATHMEY

AND

C. WALTHALL.

"THE HOUSE OF ONE FRANKLIN."

By W. H. GWATHMEY.

From Mrs. Ann M. Shepherd, an intelligent and worthy member of our Church, who is now sixty-seven years of age, I learn that the house of *"one Franklin"* in which the First Church was constituted, in the year 1780, stood at the Northeast corner of Carrington and Pink Streets, near the present Northeast suburbs of the city. Her oldest sister, Mrs. Tyler, long since dead, formerly resided on the adjoining lot, and in visiting her sister, she has many a time seen the Franklin House, and has been in it.

She describes it as a small wooden building, containing a single room, of scarcely more than sixteen or eighteen feet in dimensions, with a smaller shed-room attached on the western side, and a chimney in the middle. The lot fronted about forty feet on the north side of Carrington Street, and the house was on the Southeast corner of the lot. It is a part of the property of the estate of the late Bernhard—commonly known as " Barney "—Briel, where he resided for many years before his death, which occurred in the year 1875, at eighty-two years of age. Some of these facts I ascertained by personal inspection of the premises, which I recently visited with her. Mrs. Briel — the widow of Mr. " Barney Briel"—is still residing on the old homestead, and is the youngest sister of Mrs. Shepherd. She is a Baptist, and a lady of much energy, which she exhibited, in the management of business matters, previously to her husband's death. She conducted me to the spot, which is now enclosed as a part of her flower garden. She fully substantiated the statement of Mrs. Shepherd, and told me further, that for many years she had in her personal possession the original Title Deeds to the property, conveyed to her husband by the heirs of Mr. Franklin; and had frequently examined them, and conversed with her husband on the subject. The house was removed only a few years before the commencement of her residence there as the second Mrs. Briel. In her earlier life, she had often seen the house, and having been in it, she remembers its appearance and character perfectly well.

The mother of these ladies, Mrs. Murray, was long a member of our Church, and died in 1850, at an advanced age. From her and their uncle, Mr. Thomas Murray, who was considerably older, and who joined the Church while yet an apprentice boy, they derived what they know of the matter.

Mr. Murray died about 1831 or 1832, at sixty-one years of age. He was an earnest and active Christian, well posted in the early history of the Church, and enthusiastic in his interest in it.

Mrs. Shepherd states that she has often listened to the animated conversations between him and her mother on the subject. Her father and uncle remembered well events that transpired during the Revolutionary War, and one of their sisters was then a grown woman. The testimony of other elderly persons who have resided in the vicinity in years long past, is of the same tenor.

One venerable and trustworthy gentleman, Mr. Wm. Allen,—now in his eightieth year,—states that he was intimately acquainted with Mr. Wm. Franklin, the only son of Mr. John

Franklin, and that he distinctly remembers him as having served his time with Mr. Thos. Diddep, a famous tailor of those days, and that he never knew a more genial or kindly-hearted man, though neither he, or his only sister, Mrs. Haywood, were ever professors of religion, as far as can be ascertained. He remembers once attending a wedding at this house, then occupied and owned by Wm. Franklin, by inheritance, from his father.

The main facts as to the identification of the "Franklin House" and its location seem not to be disputed: and it is presumed that there need be no future doubt or question on the subject.

I learn that besides Mr. *John Franklin*, at whose house the Church was constituted; Mr. *John Williams*, grandfather of our sister, Miss Susan Williams—lately deceased, but well-known to many of us; *Mrs. Lewis*, great-grandmother of our sister, Mrs. Julius A. Hobson; and *Mrs. Martha Miller*, grandmother of Mrs. Shepherd,—were constituent members. At the house of Mrs. Miller, situated near the corner of Eighteenth and Venable Streets, the Church met for worship. For how long a period it is not known. Probably sometimes also in other private houses in the vicinity—and subsequently in the Hall over the Market House on Seventeenth and Main Streets. Mrs. Shepherd states that her mother told her, that she had many times attended the service there, and that the Church while worshipping there had been favored with a gracious outpouring of the Holy Spirit upon the people, and a more or less extensive revival of religion.

And finally, it is stated, that the services continued to be held in this Hall, till the meeting-house on Cary Street was built and ready for the occupancy of the Church.

HOUSES OF WORSHIP.

By C. WALTHALL.

THE first house of worship, erected by the Church, was located on the north side of D, or Cary Street, at a point near the centre, between Second and Third Streets. Some think it was west of the line that divides the two quarter sections of the square. The assessor's book of 1798, 1799, and 1800, places it on lot 659, which lot is east of that line.

The question has been raised whether the Church owned the ground on which the house stood. The assessor so regarded it; for, on his book, under the head of proprietors, the lot is charged to the "Baptist Meeting." The same assessor transferred this lot in 1801 to another party. This indicates that the Church sold it at some time between 1798 and 1801. Of course, nothing can be learned from the assessor's books as to the exact position of the house. But that he assessed the Church with that lot is clear; and as there is circumstantial evidence that it was not on the eastern side, we place it at or near the western boundary of the lot. It seems probable that it stood somewhat removed from the street, or highway. At this late day, no more minute description of the house can be given than that quoted by Dr. Burrows from Mr. Mordecai, on page 65 of this volume. It was, doubtless, very economically built. The Church had only a few members; and they, we suppose, were in limited circumstances. It is not unlikely that members of the Church built the house by their own personal labor. Unpretending as it was, still it was a *sanctuary*, where much fervent prayer was made for blessings which we enjoy to-day.

But we take leave of this spot, and follow this devoted band to their new church-house, of which we may speak more understandingly.

The next house of worship was erected on ground presented to the Church by Dr. Philip Turpin, of Chesterfield County, in 1802, at the northeast corner of H, or Broad, and College Streets. As first built, this house stood at some distance from both Broad and College Streets, and also from the eastern boundary of the lot. Its dimensions were about forty by forty feet, with a recess on the west side large enough for a small gallery, and possibly a corresponding recess and gallery on the east side.

In process of time it became necessary to increase its seating capacity. The house was enlarged by extending the eastern wing, and by adding to the front or southern side. Thus the house was brought near to the line of Broad street. There are no records extant that show when these additions were made.

From the records of the Court we learn that in or about the year 1819 a second deed was made by Dr. Turpin to this lot. The objects were to correct the first deed, it having been discovered that there was some discrepancy between the quantity of ground conveyed and the actual quantity the lot contained; and to correct some irregularity in the trusteeship. It is probable that this discovery resulted from a survey of the ground then made with a view to enlarging the house. If so, these additions were made at or about the time this amended deed was granted. This, however, is conjectural.

In 1827, the Church, receiving large accessions, found it necessary to increase still further the capacity of the house. This was done by adding twenty feet to the west wing. This being accomplished, the house assumed the form and dimensions which it had when pulled down, in 1876, to build on the same site the First African Church.

In 1838, the Church, then composed of whites and colored members, had so increased, that the house, capacious as it was, could not hold even the membership, when there was a full attendance.

This necessitated the adoption of some means of relief. The subject was discussed from time to time till 1840, when all necessary arrangements were made for the white and colored members to separate. The former proposed to the latter, to relinquish the house to them, on certain conditions stipulated. The proposition being accepted by the colored members, the whites purchased the eligible lot at the northwest corner of Broad and Twelfth Streets, on which they erected a new and spacious edifice. It was dedicated October 17th, 1841. The house was designed by Mr. Thomas U. Walter, of Philadelphia. The several parts of the work were done as follows: the stone work by Alvey Take, the brick by Jesse Williams, the carpentering by John and Samuel

Freeman, the roofing by D. and C. R. Weller, the upholstering by John D. Smith.

In 1858, the building was enlarged by adding to the rear some thirteen or fourteen feet. In the spring of 1868, with a view of making room for the organ, which the Church had agreed to put in the house, further alterations were made in the rear.

In 1870, the attendance, especially of young children of the Sunday-school, having increased, the room now known as the Side Chapel, was built at the northwest corner of the main building.

The whole cost of this house of worship, embracing the original, and all subsequent enlargement, aggregates about $49,000. Several thousand dollars had been spent in repairing, renewing furniture, and repainting. Not less than $55,000 have been spent on the house. This is the House in which we to-day assemble. May it stand, as it promises, for ages to come, and within its walls, may multitudes be fitted for dwelling in *the house* not made with hands, eternal in the heavens.

OFFICERS OF THE CHURCH.

BY

J. B. WATKINS.

OFFICERS OF THE CHURCH.

THE discourses of the morning have given adequate attention to the Pastors of the Church. My task is limited to sketches of other officers. Propriety suggests that these delineations be devoted chiefly to the dead. The future annalist will do justice to the memory of the men now moving among us.

Among the living, we have had, as *Clerks*, Christopher Walthall and John C. Williams; as *Treasurers*, James P. Tyler and James L. Apperson. The present Clerk is D. O. Davis. The present Treasurers, R. B. Lee and Wm. H. Tatum. The former Deacons, now living, are John C. Stanard, Geo. J. Sumner, J. B. Watkins, U. G. Hoyt, and John Hart. The present Deacons are L. R. Warren, J. B. Hill, R. S. Sadler, O. H. Chalkley, William F. Harwood, William G. Dandridge, A. P. Fox,

William H. Gwathmey, Robert H. Bosher, and Christopher Walthall.

These sketches must be brief. Those of the earlier officers will be less complete because of lack of information. Greater detail will be given to those living later, and better known, and whose terms of service were longer.

Herbert C. Thompson and Thomas J. Glenn were the earliest Clerks of whom we have any record. They were faithful officers and good men. The former withdrew from the Church in 1820 to assist in the formation of the Second Church; and the latter, in 1832, united with those who held the views of Mr. Alexander Campbell.

David Roper Crane and John Humes McCarthy served the Church as Clerks, each about five years. The former from 1848 to 1853, the latter from 1854 to 1858. They were lovely and pleasant in their lives, and in their death, they were not long divided.

David R. Crane was the eldest son of James C. Crane, a Church Deacon, of whom mention will presently be made. He was gifted in prayer, and in public address; and was favored with a fine voice, and excellent musical talent. He was an efficient Sunday-school teacher, a conscientious, lowly Christian; and as a recorder and keeper of the proceedings of the Church he had no superior. He died of consumption in 1853, leaving a young wife and tender babe to lament their loss.

Failing fast, while with the family of his father-in-law near this city, his wish to be brought home to die was gratified. As he calmly passed away, in 1855, he murmured: "accepted in the beloved; the will of the Lord."

John H. McCarthy was a victim of the same fell disease. At the age of twenty-seven years, he fell asleep in Jesus in 1859, calmly directing arrangements for his funeral, and giving mementoes of affection to weeping ones at his bedside. His life was an appropriate prelude to such a death. His official duties were faithfully and satisfactorily performed.

Without regard to chronological order, the following sketches are of deceased Deacons:

Robert Hyde, Onan Ellyson, and Charles H. Hyde were among the earliest of whom we have any record. When Robert Hyde was appointed Deacon is not known, owing to the loss of the first record books. Mr. Ellyson was made Deacon in 1825. Mr. Charles H. Hyde, a son of Robert, entered the deaconry in

1827. These three brethren left the Church in 1832, and assisted in the formation of the Disciples Church, now worshipping in the building at the corner of Seventh and Grace Streets. The Hydes have descendants in some of our churches, and Mr. Ellyson has two well-known sons, who are members of the Second Baptist Church of this city.

Anthony R. Thornton was a Deacon of the Church until his death in 1828. The length of his official term is unknown. Probably it was twenty-five or thirty years. He was a conspicuous man in the community, and exerted a good influence. He is represented as tall and commanding in person. The office of Deputy Marshall of the United States Court, under General J. W. Pegram, was filled by him. His associates, now living, bear testimony to his interest and usefulness in the Church.

Peter Winston united with the Church in 1826. He was an honored Deacon, perhaps for ten or twelve years. Active and attentive to duty, genial and pleasant in manner, he was universally esteemed in the community, and in the Church. He died in the neighboring county of Chesterfield in the year 1841, the funeral services taking place from this Church.

Prof. Charles H. Winston, one of his sons, is a member of our Church. Samuel Hardgrove was a Deacon of the Church from 1827 to 1829, and continued an esteemed member until his death in 1862.

Zachary Lewis was a Deacon from 1827 to 1833, when he withdrew from the Church by letter. His subsequent history is unknown. He is represented as a faithful Christian and officer, with an unblemished reputation. Simon Frayser was a Deacon from 1829 until his death in 1834, in the forty-third year of his age. Grateful witness is borne to the faithful and acceptable manner in which he discharged his official and Christian duties. He was peculiarly gifted in prayer. The eloquent Mr. Kerr often called on him to lead the supplications of the assembly, at the close of his thrilling sermons. Of fine personal appearance, and engaging manners, he was very popular with all classes of the community, and dispensed a generous hospitality. He has in this city a well-known son, identified with the origin and growth of the Venable Street Baptist Church.

F. J. Lewis, Joseph Starke, and B. W. Walthall were elected Deacons in 1833. Mr. Lewis served about two years, and was dismissed from the Church by letter, and removed to the West. Mr. Starke served about the same length of time, and withdrew from the Church to assume the duties of a gospel minister. Mr. Walthall served as a Deacon four years. He then moved to Mississippi, where he maintained a high character, and reared an interesting family. At an advanced age he still lives, and is a member of the Episcopal Church. During their official terms, these brethren were consistent and efficient Christians. Mr. Starke as a minister has received to-day a deserved tribute at the hands of Dr. Burrows.

W. E. Clopton and J. Harvie Temple served as Deacons in 1835, about one year each. They were then dismissed by letters and left the city. Mr. Clopton was a brother of an able jurist, the late Judge John B. Clopton, and is represented as a faithful officer and Christian. Similar testimony is borne to the character and services of Mr. Temple. They left the Church and the city about the same time. Mr. Temple resumed his residence here, and died in the year 1871. He has an aged sister, and a nephew bearing his name, who are members of this Church. John Farrar united with the

Church by baptism in 1842. He was elected a Deacon in 1848, and served for ten years, when he died in Richmond in 1858, lamented by a large circle of relatives, friends, and brethren. He occupied prominent business positions, and was at one time in prosperous circumstances.

Richard Reins was born on the 19th of December, 1797, in the county of King William, of wealthy parents, but was early left an orphan, and stripped of his patrimony. At the age of seventeen he entered into business in this city. He united with the Church by baptism in 1826. In 1833, he was made a Deacon, and discharged the duties of the office for thirty-eight years most faithfully, until his death in Richmond in 1871. His nature was generous, ardent, and resolute. He did nothing by halves. Into every enterprise or effort he threw his whole soul. By industry, he accumulated a comfortable estate, from which he gave liberally to every good cause. No agent of any important enterprise appealed to him in vain. His friends sometimes deemed him extravagant in his gifts. The distinguished Luther Rice, his friend and frequent guest, for whom one of his sons is named, received from him a donation for Columbian College, which was deemed so large, that a pastor present exclaimed: "Brother Reins, the Baptists should certainly see to it that you never suffer want." His decision, promptness, and dispatch were remarkable. Serious mistakes he doubtless made, but as Bourrienne said of Napoleon, he went forward with so much celerity and vigor that he often ran them down and cleared them. He was a confiding friend, and a hospitable host. Sincere and honest himself, he lost heavily by unsuspecting faith in others. Adversity at last overtook him. The infirmities of age, and losses and crosses wrecked his earthly hopes. But he had higher hopes, to which he clung to the last. In weakness and depression they cheered him, and in the supreme hour they sustained him, until his freed spirit fled to the realms of the blest. One who knew and loved him writes: "A warmer, truer, braver heart never beat in human breast. While many seem to be more religious than they are, Mr. Reins was more so than he outwardly appeared." He was one of the Building Committee for the erection of this house of worship.

James Sizer was born in Caroline County, Virginia, on the 18th of January, 1784. Like Reins, he embarked in business here in early life, and amassed an independent fortune. In 1827, he was baptized into the fellowship of the Church, and two years later was made a Deacon, and discharged the duties of the office for thirty-eight years, until his death in 1867. His nature was not to lead, and to take a prominent part in the affairs of the Church.

He was quiet, unobtrusive, uniformly consistent, and interested in whatever pertained to the interests of Christ's Kingdom. As Treasurer of the Church, and member of the Building Committee which superintended the erection of this house, he was energetic, attentive, and liberal. At length financial embarassments overtook him. He lost the gains of years. But his integrity was never questioned, and on his reputation no blemish rested. He submissively met his reverses, and retained the respect of every one. His life extended to four-score and four years. Touching at his birth the close of one revolution and at his death the close of another, he linked together the experiences of four generations. He anticipated death, and with entire composure awaited its approach. Among his papers the following was found, written with his own hand, on his eightieth birth-day: "The word of God, the Old and New Testament, are precious to read, contemplate, and meditate upon. Read 19th Psalm of David. But my trust is in a risen Saviour, Jesus Christ, who came to seek and to save sinners such as I am. 18th January, 1864. Jas. Sizer." Thus sustained, he trustfully yielded his long life into the hands of his Saviour on the 18th March, 1867. He was a member of the Board of Trustees of the Baptist Seminary, from which our College sprang.

Archibald Thomas was born March 28th, 1796, in Caroline County, Virginia, where he passed his childhood and youth. In early manhood he began business in Richmond, which was successfully pursued until he became financially independent. He was converted and entered the Church in 1826, and in February of the following year was made Deacon, filling the office for thirty years, until the date of his death. He was a member and the Treasurer of the Foreign Mission Board of the Southern Baptist Convention, from its formation until near the close of his life. Not confining himself to the technical routine of duty, he frequently in his correspondence with the missionaries, addressed to them words of affectionate sympathy and interest. He was a member of the

Building Committee for the erection of this Church and of the Board of Trustees of the Baptist Seminary.

On the Lord's Day just preceding his death, in April 1861, a collection was expected to be taken in the Church for the Foreign Mission Board. The disturbance in public affairs prevented it. That afternoon the Treasurer of the Board, visiting him, received from him a twenty-dollar bill, which he had intended to give at the collection. No man was ever more hospitable. In his pleasant home, many of the most esteemed and eminent members and ministers of the denomination were courteously entertained. Mr. Thomas was not demonstrative. To be appreciated, he had to be known. But when known, he was found to be genial, true, and loving in every relation of life. He attracted by no art of manner, but grew upon his friends, and bound them to him with more than " triple bands of steel." To duty he inflexibly adhered, and as a church member was a strict disciplinarian. Not that he loved his fellows less, but the purity of Christ's Church more. Though his health was feeble for some months, his death was sudden and unexpected. On the night of the 1st of May, 1861, he retired to rest, with no alarming symptoms. The quick ear of his wife caught sounds of labored breathing. The deadly dart defied all remedies, and in a few moments he passed away. For nearly a score of years, the happiness of heaven has been his. But a few weeks since, his glorified spirit doubtless derived fresh infusion of joy, by the blissful entrance into rest of the noble wife of his youth and manhood.

James C. Crane was born on the 7th of September, 1803, in Newark, New Jersey. Early left fatherless, he was carefully trained by a pious mother and elder sister. The latter taught him such apothegms as the following, on which seemed modeled his character: "Learn to be independent." "Never lean on anybody." "Command the respect of others by deserving it." "Disdain all subterfuges." "Adhere conscientiously to truth and right." "Above all, make the Bible your constant study and guide." At the age of sixteen Mr. Crane came to Richmond, entering his elder brother's store as a clerk. He joined the Second Baptist Church, then in charge of Rev. James B. Taylor. At the age of nineteen he thus writes to a brother in New Jersey: "The Second Church have been building a new meeting-house. We had to pay our money pretty smartly. But what we have is not our own, and we ought to recollect that we are but stewards, and will have to give an account of our stewardship at the last day." What golden words for a youth of nineteen! How becoming would they be for the youths of to-day! In 1839, business interests took him to Baltimore, where he remained about two years. He then returned to Richmond and united with this Church. He was elected Deacon about the year 1842. In business, as in everything, he was a man of wondrous energy, accuracy, and decision. Dr. Jeter said of him: "His word was accounted his bond, and his bond as the bill of a specie paying bank." His type of manhood was *positive, direct*. Gentle reproofs of the profane, kindly invitations to young men to enter the Church and Sunday-school, and generous gifts to every good cause, were some of his methods of doing good. As a hearer of the word, he was never listless. He sought "first the kingdom of God," and allowed no secular affairs to detain him from public worship, the prayer-meeting, or the Board Conference. He possessed striking versatility of talent. One seeing him leading the singing, would say, "he ought to teach music." Superintending the Sunday-school, he was deemed just the man for a Sunday-school Missionary. Participating in Board deliberations, he seemed admirably adapted to a controlling secretaryship. Expounding the word, and leading the devotional meeting, many declared the gospel ministry his manifest vocation. The problem of his devotement to this high calling, he long and anxiously pondered. That his decision was conscientious, none can doubt. The key-note of his life is touched in a letter to his sister: "*Oh that my heart and thoughts might be chained to the glory of God!* Shall I, at the last day, behold one on the left hand, whom I might have warned, or been the instrument of saving?" Oh that such solemn inquiries might be made by all of us! He was a fast and efficient friend of Foreign Missions. Abundant evidences from his own pen, and from others, might be adduced in proof of his great usefulness and consecration as Deacon and Sunday-school Superintendent. It is no disparagement of others to say, that no man, within any equal period of his connection with this Church, ever exerted an influence so wide, deep, and beneficent. But now that brave and buoyant heart is to bow; that agile form is to fail; those large lustrous eyes are to weep. His gifted sons are removed to the Cemetery; disease smites his own frame. Consumption, that fearful scourge, which bore away his noble boys, stands at his own door. Hear him under these trials: "We can glorify our Lord more by a quiet submissive spirit under suffering than in any other way. 'For I reckon that the sufferings of this present time, are not worthy to be compared with the glory that shall be revealed in us.'"

The Red Sulphur Springs, and the milder airs of the southern seaside were sought in vain. At the comparatively early age of fifty-three he came home, and calmly composed himself to die. A few hours before his death, a friend said to him: "Brother Crane, in looking over your past life, do you see anything in its general course that you would change if you could?" Remaining silent for a few moments, and then raising his head, he replied: "*As to its main current, no!*" A noble confession in the honest hour of death. Breathing a blessing upon his faithful wife and only child—a lad of twelve years—and whispering after paroxysms of pain, "Kind friends; kind Redeemer, I can trust him; Come, Lord Jesus," he gently passed to the better land, in March, 1856. Never have I seen, on any similar occasion, a larger or more sorrowful assembly than the one gathered within these walls, on that early spring evening, to do honor to the memory of this noble man. Business circles sent their representatives, and ministers of all persuasions were here to mingle their tears with those of his family and brethren. His pastor, Dr. Burrows, from whose excellent memoir of him much of this sketch is compiled, preached a touching discourse from the fitting words: "Thou shalt be missed, because thy seat will be empty," 1 Samuel 20: 18. Aye, he was missed. "Blessed are the dead who die in the Lord, for they rest from their labors, and their works do follow them."

Rev. Dr. M. D. Hoge, of the Presbyterian Church, an inmate with him of the same house, said: "Seldom have I witnessed such a life, and such a death-bed scene." Yes, dear brother, thou art missed * * but thou art not missed from the ransomed in heaven. Thou holdest a place there which never can be empty.

The late Rev. Dr. George Woodbridge, of the Episcopal Church, said: "Yesterday, when I heard of his death, I felt much as a soldier feels on the field of battle, who turns to find a beloved comrade fallen."

Our own lamented and revered Rev. Richard Fuller, D. D., closed a letter of just eulogy of him, with the words: "Let me die the death of the righteous, and let my last end be like his." Literally, was the petition granted. Both now "walk in white, for they were worthy."

Than Reins, Sizer, Thomas, and Crane, four men can scarcely be found who combined in their characters traits more dissimilar and divergent. Reins was more rapid and resolute in will than either of his three compeers. Than either, he was better fitted to be the leader of a forlorn hope, or to brave the perils of an exigency. For patient tenderness, prudent procedure, and kind conciliation, Sizer excelled them all. In clear judgment, deep penetration, and inflexible firmness, Thomas surpassed Reins and Sizer, and was the equal of Crane. In Crane was happily embraced, in almost exact equipoise, the rushing energy of Reins, the calm composure of Sizer, and the stern stability of Thomas. The aim and effort of each was the advancement of Christ's Kingdom and the honored growth of the Church of which they were members. Thus does God graciously give to his Church men with "diversities of gifts, but the same spirit."

HISTORY OF THE SUNDAY-SCHOOL.

BY

C. WALTHALL.

HISTORY OF THE SUNDAY-SCHOOL.

THE time when the Sunday-school of the First Baptist Church began is not definitely known. From the best information obtainable, it started in or about 1817. It is said that the school commenced with four teachers and six scholars. This seems probable. The number at first, was certainly very small.

Accepting as true the statement that it commenced with four teachers, it becomes a matter of interest to learn who they were. The writer thinks the honor of this precedence may be safely given to Mrs. Frances Greenhow, Mrs. Maria O. Marshall, Miss Virginia Ratcliffe and Miss Jane C. Charlton. Who the scholars were he cannot say. Other teachers entered the school soon after. Among these may be named: Miss Rebecca Williams, Miss Mary Nelson, Miss Sarah Ross, and Miss Sarah Hillyard, Philip Spare, and William Dabney. Of the scholars who were in the school, at an early period, may be mentioned: Miss Martha F. Nowell, Misses Elizabeth and Susan Coghill, Miss Jane Daniel, Miss Sarah Grant. Of the four teachers first mentioned, it may be remarked briefly: Mrs. Greenhow continued, an active member of the Church, till June, 1828, when she transferred her membership to the Second Church; Mrs. Marshall became the wife of Mr. George Roper, and united with others in the formation of the Second Church, in 1820; Miss Virginia Ratcliffe, whose life is fragrant to this day in the memory of the older members, remained single during life, was conspicuously pious and devoted, and after a long and useful life, in the service of the Master, in connection with this Church, went to her reward in 1852; Miss Charlton, became the wife of Rev. Henry Keeling, and assisted him in the conduct of a school, which he taught for some years in Richmond. Mrs. Keeling was noted for intelligence, piety, gentility of manner, and scrupulous neatness in her person. She was a teacher in the school at a later period than either of the others. She died in 1860.

Herbert C. Thomson, in whose school-room the Sunday-school seems to have started, was the first Superintendent.

In addition to superintending the school, Mr. Thomson led the music of the Church and filled the office of Church Clerk till 1820, when he, with fourteen other members, was dismissed to form the Second Church, of which he was made Clerk. He seems to have been admirably suited for the office—his chirography was uniform and neat, and his composition was good. After some time of active service in the Second Church, Mr. Thomson, being impressed that it was his duty to preach the gospel, was, after trial of his gifts, licensed in 1823, and in February, 1828, he was regularly ordained. Soon thereafter, he removed from the city and, nothing is known of his subsequent life.

Who immediately succeeded Mr. Thomson as Superintendent, is not certainly known. The Church Records from the time he left to January, 1825, being lost, no information can be gotten from that source, of what took place in the Sunday-school during the intervening four years. From those preserved, it appears that the Church took action in regard to the Sunday-school at various times down to 1829, as follows:

In May, 1827, Miss Virginia Ratcliffe and Miss Betsey Philips were appointed teachers in the Sunday-school.

In June, 1827, Mr. Joseph Woodson was appointed Assistant Superintendent, in place of John G. Davis, resigned.

In the same month, Mr. James Sizer was appointed Assistant Superintendent, and three persons, Johnson, Laneve and Frost were appointed teachers.

In September, 1827, N. H. Davis and James Thomas were appointed teachers.

In June, 1828, the Church appointed a committee to act in concert with the Richmond and Manchester Sunday-School Union in the celebration of the day of National Independence.

In May, 1829, the Superintendent was directed to report to the Church the condition of the Sunday-school and suggest such improvements as he might think necessary for the further success of the institution.

In June following, 1829, Mr. Joseph Woodson resigned as Superintendent. He must have at some prior time been promoted from Assistant to Principal. Mr. Sizer, heretofore mentioned as an officer of the school, was also an officer of the Church, and will be noticed as such by another.

The other two, Davis and Woodson, were among the number who went out from the

Church in 1832 to form what is now known as the Seventh Street Christian Church. To that Church, we leave the duty of finishing their record, when it comes to celebrate its half-centennial, which they propose to do.

On accepting Woodson's resignation, in June, 1829, the Church adopted the following:

"*Resolved*, That we as a Church do now withdraw all connection from the Sabbath-school so as to give place for the formation of a society to which the whole management of the school is referred."

A Committee was appointed to settle the Treasurer's account.

This seems to be an entire abandonment by the Church of the policy which had governed it from its first recognition of the school, which some have said was in 1816. But the old mother seemed to entertain some regard for her cast-off child; for she allowed, on two occasions thereafter, collections to be taken in the Church in aid of the school. Let us not harshly judge her, but wait to see if she does not right herself as she pursues her way.

The next known Superintendent was Mr. Archibald Thomas. When and how he was chosen does not appear. In view of the action of the Church just recited, he must have been appointed by the school, and probably very soon after that action was taken. If so, he was the immediate successor of Woodson, in 1829.

During Mr. Thomas' term of service, two young men, Joseph S. Walthall and John O. Turpin, entered upon a course of study preparatory to the gospel ministry. On the resignation of Mr. Thomas, in 1832 or 1833, Richard N. Herndon and Joseph S. Walthall, then at the Seminary on the Brook Pike, jointly superintended the school, during one session of the Seminary, and until they left for other fields of labor.

The school was now left almost entirely in the hands of those who had just before come into the Church. The choice of a Superintendent fell on the writer. Being unanimously called, and relying on the hearty co-operation of those around him whom he knew to be zealous and devoted, he ventured, in humble trust in God, to undertake the office. He continued in that service till 1841. The school was held, where it had been for a number of years before, in the basement under the east wing of the old house of worship. Contracted and otherwise unsuitable, this place could not well accommodate more than sixty or seventy pupils. The average attendance of scholars, during the whole time the school met in this place, ranged from fifty to sixty. Under very propitious circumstances, eighty to one hundred occasionally attended. A few months before the close of this officer's term, viz., in May, 1841, the school was transferred to the basement of the new house of worship. During his term also occurred several interesting events. Miss Henrietta Hall, a teacher, who became the wife of Rev. J. L. Shuck, Robert Davenport, and Samuel C. Clopton went out from the school, as missionaries to the heathen; and Wm. M. Gaskins, J. G. Councill and A. P. Repiton gave themselves to the work of the ministry.

To one other thing that occurred during this time special attention is called. In April, 1834, the Church adopted the following:

"*Resolved*, that George W. Atkinson, H. J. Crawford, J. L. Apperson, Elijah Johnson, Robert H. Bosher, W. P. Mann, Geo. L. Wright, L. D. Walker and C. Walthall be appointed a committee to conduct the Sabbath-school connected with the Church; that they be empowered to chose their own officers, to add to their number, from time to time, such others as may be necessary ; and that they make a report of their proceedings and the state of the School annually to the Church."

In 1841, C. Walthall resigned the Superintendency, in order that the School might avail itself of the services of Mr. James C. Crane, who was at the time a teacher in the School, and whose superior qualifications were universally recognized. He was elected to the office. Under Mr. Crane's management the School had the advantage of the removal of the Church to its new house. The attendance of scholars averaged about two hundred and fifty during his term of six years.

A. H. Sands, V. A. Gaskill and P. S. Henson became preachers.

In 1847, Mr. Crane resigned, and Mr. James Thomas, Jr., was elected as his successor. Mr. Thomas' term of about nineteen years was an eventful one, embracing as it did the whole period of the late civil war. For several years after Mr. Thomas took charge, there was no very material change in the attendance. Afterwards it reached a height of prosperity never before attained by this or any other School of the city. Over five hundred pupils were sometimes present. J. Hume, Jr., Geo. Wm. Keesee, Wm. H. Williams, W. S. Ryland, Lansing Burrows, and the Superintendent's own son, W. D. Thomas, went from the School to preach. When the war came on, or soon after, Mr. Thomas moved from the city and was seldom present during the war.

The school, like other enterprises of the day, felt the withering effects of that exciting period, and became much demoralized. It was kept up as best it could be under such circumstances. Mr. R. H. Bosher, who was Mr. Thomas' Assistant, had charge during this time and till 1866, when he was elected the successor of Mr. Thomas.

Under Mr. Bosher's superintendency the school regained its former standing and maintained, through his tenure of office, a steady, healthy condition. During that time two young men, W. O. Thomas and H. A. Tupper, Jr., went out as candidates for the ministry.

Mr. Bosher's official relations to the school terminated, January, 1878, when Mr. Wm. Miles Turpin, the present incumbent, was elected Superintendent. As Mr. Turpin has yet to make, in part at least, his record, we only express our ardent desire that it may be a bright one—exceeding in good fruitage that of his predecessors. In one respect he occupies a peculiar position. When the next centennial history of the School is written, his name will stand at the close of the one century and at the beginning of the other.

This suggests that all of us who are engaged in this work should remember that we commence to-day to make the second century's history. Let every one see to it that the foundation is well laid.

JETER MEMORIAL.

PAPER
By J. L. M. CURRY.

ADDRESSES
By J. B. HAWTHORNE and WM. E. HATCHER.

RELATION OF THE CHURCH TO EDUCATION.

By J. L. M. CURRY.

The undersigned, appointed to collect facts in reference to the connection of the First Church with the cause of education, regrets that all efforts made by him have been nearly fruitless.

The minutes of the General Association show that in 1833 Elder John Kerr, the Pastor of this Church, was the President of the Virginia Baptist Education Society, out of which grew the Seminary, and afterwards Richmond College. In 1833, the Treasurer and five of the Managers of this Society were members of this Church. Ever since, the Education Board has had representatives from this Church, and has received generous contributions. Richmond College, in its Trustees and Faculty, has depended somewhat on the Church. Every effort made to endow the College has received efficient help from our membership, and now this is the only Church in the State which has a scholarship in the College for the education of the sons of Baptist ministers.

Richmond Female Institute, throughout its entire history, has found in the First Church zealous and liberal friends and patrons, as well as Trustees and Teachers.

The Southern Baptist Theological Seminary has from its origin been also the constant recipient of First Church benefactions in its efforts for endowment, as well as in special efforts for the support of students and Faculty.

This Church has steadily recognized that the gospel was intended to vitalize and mould every energy and form of human activity, so that man's whole being may be brought into thorough accord with the will of God. For Christianizing society, a most important place must be assigned to education. The impulse, spontaneous and general and honorable, to commemorate in some permanent manner the life and services of Dr. Jeter, took, after earnest consultation, the form of completing the Richmond College building and having therein a "Jeter Memorial Hall," in which should be deposited, along with his bust or picture, the books and manuscripts which Dr. Jeter, in his will, bequeathed to the College. The First Church must feel a double interest in such an enterprise. The College has been a special favorite with the Church, and in 1872 she gave up her Pastor to carry on the great memorial enterprise. Dr. Jeter, for many years, was our Pastor, and no Church can cherish a livelier or more grateful recollection of his laborious and holy ministry. The First Church can, therefore, most feelingly unite with the Baptists of Virginia in doing, in the manner proposed, proper honor to one so closely connected with her history. We can also, in celebrating our centennial, set up our Ebenezer by doing something permanently beneficent in our Master's cause.

The Church can well join sister churches, and thus broaden sympathies and bring the brotherhood into closer fellowship and sympathy.

J. L. M. CURRY,
Committee.

ADDRESS.

By J. B. HAWTHORNE.

Nothing is more commendable than the respect and veneration which mankind have for the old. In the earlier and purer days of the Greek Republic, when an old man entered a crowded assembly, men of every rank and station rose to do him reverence. The proudest tree that lifts its leafy head above us awakens no such emotions in our breasts as those which we experience in looking upon the ivy-mantled trunk of an old withered and wasted oak.

Looking back, to-day, over the history of a Church festooned with the associations of a hundred years, our hearts throb with feelings far more profound and sacred than those which are excited when we survey the gilded grandeur of some modern institution.

We are old: but we have not called you together to tax your sympathy for something that is tottering under the infirmities and burdens of age. We do not call upon you to help us to conceal the ravages of time—to do for us what the tender ivy does, when she flings a green and glossy mantle over a crumbling ruin.

No. The youngest thing in Richmond to-day is this venerable Mother of Churches. She is surrounded by a family of healthy, vigorous, and accomplished daughters, of whom she is duly proud; but in buoyancy, hopefulness, energy, and enterprise—in everything that constitutes beauty, strength, and progress, she is more than a match for the best of them. She is old only in years. There is not a wrinkle upon her face, nor a silver thread among the gold. In no respect has she declined. I trust that her response, to-night, to the calls of a noble enterprise, will demonstrate that she retains both the ability and the disposition to do great things for God and the world.

We have had laid before us to-day, in the able papers read by Drs. Burrows and Thomas, the work which our fathers accomplished. We have entered into their labors. We are born to an inheritance bequeathed to us by their toils and tears. We, who now live, are heirs of all the ages that have preceded ours. Nothing shows more clearly man's superiority to the brutes than his ability to profit by the experience and wisdom of those who have gone before him. In studying the history and the habits of the various animals around us, we are impressed with the fact that they have made no improvement. The bee builds honey-comb to-day, just as his ancestors in the wilderness of Judea built two thousand years ago. The eagle of to-day is no wiser than his progenitors who made their nests among the Cedars of Lebanon. The beavers construct their dams just as they made them ages ago. Instinct makes no progress. But intelligence grows. The wisdom of the past accumulates for men into a capital for the present, and the thoughts of one generation pass into and fructify in the next.

This great earth, on which we stand to-day, surrounded by so many objects that please the eye, and delight the soul, was brought to its present state through different creative periods, each embracing millions of years. Stratum was laid upon stratum, creation was added to creation, until God looked out from the heavens and pronounced it good, complete. Just so it has been with the successive generations of men. They have not been simply repetitions of each other, like the generations of the lower animals; but each as it has passed away has left some new stratum of knowledge, wisdom, and experience to be added as its instalment to the patrimony of the race. We are wiser and richer than our fathers, because we come after them, and inherit their wisdom and wealth.

> "We walk abroad and gather as our own,
> The precious harvests which the dead have sown."

The secrets which Galileo discovered when he turned his rude telescope to the heavens, and the laws which Newton so ably expounded, are elementary principles in our education. The progress of learning since their day has placed us in possession of a world of knowledge, of which they never dreamed.

Who doubts that the Church of the Lord Jesus is richer to-day than it was a hundred years ago! By all that was accomplished by such men as the Wesleys, Whitefield, Carey, and Judson; by all that was ripe in the wisdom, grand in the eloquence, and noble in the lives of such men as Thornwell, Frederick W. Robertson, Francis Wayland, and Richard Fuller; by all the victories that have been won for Christ in battles with pagan superstition and infidel philosophy, the Church is richer, stronger, and better equipped for holy warfare to-day than it was a century ago.

"I have sent you to reap that whereon you bestowed no labor." That is our position. We stand in the midst of a harvest prepared for us by the toils of other men. We have entered into other men's labors. We are building on foundations which our fathers laid, and with a thousand helps and advantages which they never possessed. The practical question before us to-night, the question which I pray God to lay upon the conscience of every member of this Church, is, what will you do with this legacy? What will you do with the results of a hundred years of faith, and prayer, and sacrifice, and toil? Will you improve them and add to them, so that you shall leave them to those who come after you, enlarged and enriched by some new deposit of your own? or will you sit down in idleness and see them waste away and perish?

It has grown into a proverb. "The boy who begins his fortune where his father left off, will end where his father began." As a rule, inherited wealth is a title deed to sloth. Many a

Church has begun a downward career at the point when she felt that she was "rich and increased in goods, and in need of nothing." No young man will succeed in any trade or profession who aims at being simply a repetition of his father. His father ran a lumber-mill with horse-power and succeeded, grew rich; but let him attempt it in this day of progress and how signal will be his failure! His father learned music by a system of patent notes. Let him begin according to the same method, and how inglorious will be his career. Ministers and Churches must work in harmony with the spirit and wants of the age in which they live. David served his generation by unifying and extending his kingdom, and by collecting treasure for the building of the Temple. If Solomon had attempted to do just what his father did, no progress would have been made. But he entered into his father's labors: he took up his father's plan for the building of the Temple, and pursued it to a glorious consummation.

The age in which we live has problems of its own—problems which differ from those of every previous age—and we must solve them, and thus improve upon the wisdom of the past. The truths of the gospel are immutable, but the methods of presenting them must change to keep up with the progress of thought and taste. The men who centuries ago stood at the very pinnacle of pulpit power and renown, would hardly be listened to to-day. The men and women who made the first fifty years of this Church's history were noble spirits. In their own peculiar way they wrought wonders. They built honestly and solidly. But if we were to attempt a repetition of their methods, we should utterly fail to compass the work which we are expected to do. A more eloquent man than John Kerr never stood before a Richmond audience. He was the "eagle of pulpit-eloquence." Many moons will wax and wane before Virginia will produce his equal. But his was eloquence born of peculiar circumstances, that have long since passed away. The impetuosity, the wild abandon, which gave him such power over the multitude, is not the style of speech which accords with the spirit and tastes of the audiences to which some of his successors have preached.

What would become of the Sunday-school, if we should attempt to conduct it according to the fashion of our fathers? How long would it abide the ordeal of long prayers, long chapters, long lessons, long metres, and long faces?

Would it be wise to revive the Church Music of fifty years ago? I can well remember when in one of the best of our Southern Churches the sermon was usually preceded by the singing of "Hark! from the tombs a doleful sound." It was sung as a solo by one of the Deacons, whose voice was as rickety as the sentiment was plaintive. When some of our fathers were children the violin, the flute, and the bagpipe did the work which is now performed by the organ. A country pastor, occupying for the first time the pulpit of a city Church, in which such music was in vogue, made the disastrous mistake of asking the choir to "fiddle and blow the opening hymn."

Not to reproduce the past, but to develop, out of all that is good and noble in it, results that will be of greater value to the world than those which our fathers produced—that is the duty of the hour—that is the work committed to our hands. Let us take all that has come down to us from former generations of good and faithful men, and adapt it to the needs of the day in which our lives are spent. Our relation to the generation that shall come after us is just that which our fathers sustained to us. They were sowers of seed, and so are we. We reap the results of their labors, and those who follow us will gather the fruits of our faith and toils. They live in works which they left behind them, and we may project our influence into the far future by leaving upon the shores of time proofs of our love and loyalty to God. The Lord grant that we may leave to posterity as rich a heritage as has been left to us.

Standing here upon the threshold of another century of our Church's life, let us look about us and see what new enterprise we can undertake by which we may send our benediction down to those who shall write our history and celebrate our worth? We propose to make this occasion the inauguration of such an enterprise. What shall it be? Already you have answered that question. With great unanimity you have said, "The completion of the Richmond College building." You have decided to erect the other wing, and to dedicate it to the memory of the man to whom both Church and College are more indebted than to any other man living or dead.

A few months ago the sad tidings went out to the country that J. B. Jeter was dead. Deep was our grief, loud were our lamentations. While we were yet weeping over our great loss the demand was heard from every quarter —" Let his monument be built, and his epitaph be written "! The sentiment was universal, that the Baptists of Virginia ought to erect some memorial of the beautiful virtues and noble deeds that made his life a light to the world. Nothing seems to be more in harmony with the "eternal fitness of things," than that this Church, in which the prime of his manhood was spent, and where the brightest results of his ministry were realized, should take the lead of any movement to honor his name and perpetuate the memory of his worth.

Out of the very bosom of the blackness which the infidelity of this age has gathered about our blessed religion, " shines the light of holy lives, like star-beams over doubt." Among the number whose holy living have demonstrated the divinity of our faith, there is no one more worthy of mention than the man to whom this monument will be built. Phidias proposed to make a statue of Alexander out of Mount Athos, holding in one hand a beautiful river, and in the other a magnificent city. The realization of his conception would have been the supreme triumph of art. Such was the tribute of which the great sculptor felt his hero worthy.

A hero he was; but how inglorious his end! After he had climbed the dizzy heights of his ambition, and looked down upon a conquered world, he died in the midst of a shameful debauch. He was monarch of all things but himself. There is a little world within man's own bosom in which he may rise or fall. "There is an inward government of the thoughts and passions, which is an object of loftier ambition, than the possession of any earthly crown or sceptre." He who governs himself is the only *real* potentate. Such was the man whose name we propose to honor. In the presence of any temptation; under the pressure of any trial; in the midst of the most exciting scenes,—he was master of himself. He was ambitious, but he never suffered ambition to take him one inch beyond what he believed to be the line of truth, rectitude, and honor. He was passionate, but over all feeling his great will was supreme. As the rod of Moses swallowed up all the symbols of Egyptian wizardry, so did Dr. Jeter's purpose to do right consume every meaner motive and unlawful desire.

It was a custom among the Romans to place the busts of their distinguished ancestors in the vestibules of their houses, so that they might be continually reminded of their virtues and renown. History records the name of many a great Roman who had descended from families in which this custom was observed. Let us build a monument that shall keep green in the memories of our children and our children's children, the virtues of a man who was nobler than the noblest Roman.

Dr. Jeter was zealous and steadfast in his support of the cause of education. No man ever had a more just appreciation of the advantages of education to the individual, the community, and the nation. He believed that the school-master, armed with his primer, was doing more than the soldier to uphold and extend the liberties of his country. He was enthusiastic in his devotion to Richmond College. He presided at its birth. He watched over it through all the stages and struggles of its subsequent career. He prayed for it; he wrote for it; he pleaded for it; and he gave to it of his means to the very limit of his ability. He was the unflinching friend of every man who occupied a chair in its Faculty, and of every student who came there for instruction. The welfare of that Institution was among the last subjects that engaged his thoughts upon a dying bed. It is said that Livingstone was found dead upon his knees. In that posture he breathed to heaven his last prayer for benighted Africa. It would be substantially true to say that Dr. Jeter died praying for Richmond College.

How, then, can we honor his name in a manner that will more beautifully harmonize with the spirit, character, and history of the man, than by making his monument a part of the Institution he loved so well, and for which he labored so faithfully? To erect the other wing of the building and call it the "Jeter Wing;" to set apart a spacious hall in that wing and call it "The Jeter Memorial Hall;" to place within this hall his library and manuscripts, and also a life-size portrait of his majestic form,—would be a graceful and imposing tribute to his memory and a help to the College that would greatly increase its influence and patronage.

To accomplish this object, only twenty-five thousand dollars are required. If the Baptists of Virginia refuse to contribute this sum, they will prove themselves unworthy of the man who for more than fifty years bore aloft their banner in the ranks of holy war. If the old Church over whose head a century has rolled its suns away should refuse to aid in rendering this act of homage to such illustrious worth, let her blot out the memory of this day, clothe herself in sackcloth, and sit down in ashes. Let her repair to the grave of her once honored leader only to weep over the degeneracy of her spirit and the departure of her glory.

ADDRESS

By W. E. HATCHER.

M<small>Y Beloved Brethren of the First Church</small>:—You must not expect from me an elaborate address. The lateness of the hour, the richness and eloquence of the address which you have just heard from your Pastor, and the fact that Dr. Burrows is to follow me, requires me to be brief.

It was understood, I believe, that I would speak particularly in regard to the honored and lamented Dr. Jeter. To me such a task at any time would be most grateful, but happily the allusions to this famous man of God, in the addresses already made, have been so full, just, and beautiful, that but little remains to be added.

It accords with the finest impulses of our nature to honor the memory of the great and the good. Earth's noblest monuments were built in honor of those who, by living, made the world better. It is not too much to say, that within our generation no member of our Baptist brotherhood has passed away who more fully commanded respect and affection, than Dr. Jeter. Almost every point in his life and character touched the popular heart. We honor those who have made themselves—who, unhelped by fortune, have risen to distinction. This man, reared among the bleak hills of Bedford, in deepest poverty, and without good teachers, pushed upwards to the loftiest eminence. He was not that glaring, eccentric thing which shallow men call a genius, but he had an imperial mind — a mind so compact, vigorous, and clear, that he penetrated whatever he saw, and mastered whatever he touched. Do we admire high, unselfish deeds? For sixty years Dr. Jeter labored without stint for the good of others. Measured by his work, by the souls saved, the saints cheered, the poor helped, the wandering reclaimed, and the sorrowing comforted, he well merits the grateful applause of his brethren. Of all men that I have known, he had the most harmonious, consistent, and exalted character. His devotion to his Saviour was wonderful. It shaped his life and fixed his destiny.

It was no surprise, though it was profoundly touching to all hearts, when the fact was made public that this great historic Church had determined to devote her centennial thank-offering to the erection of a monument in honor of her old Pastor, Dr. Jeter. Not that you would rob Christ to exalt a man, but that you would attest your zeal for Christ by paying a splendid compliment to one of his servants. Nor is it less creditable to you that you have decided to build a monument which, while it honors the dead, shall also bless the living. Your memorial is not to be a polished shaft, not a tower of shining brass, not a costly statue, but something which will permanently associate his name with Christian learning. The conception of a Library Hall at Richmond College in memory of Dr. Jeter will attest at once your grateful recollection of the deceased, and your broad and public-spirited interest in higher education.

It only remains for me to charge you to do this work nobly and well. You never before occupied a position so conspicuous and majestic as that which you hold to-night. If you rise to the sublimity of this hour, you will add immeasurably to the glory which already crowns your Church; but if you fail now, her fame will be incurably wounded.

It has long been one of the distinctions of your Church that she has been a leader. Wise, generous, and vigorous, she has long held the lead in great movements. She has often voiced the good purposes which struggled for utterance in other churches, and often sounded the keynote which quickened others into activity. From the day that Dr. Jeter died there has been a popular clamor for a monument befitting his worth and fame. What it should be, and how it should be done, were perplexing questions. But when this Church spoke, men doubted no longer. When it was announced that your centennial gifts would be consecrated to this purpose, there was at once an assurance of success, and a readiness to help. As you have taken the front, remember that many eyes are upon you. For you to give ignobly will be to damage the enterprise which you have volunteered to champion. Failure here will be despair everywhere. You not only decide to-night what you will give, but in no mean degree, you suggest what others must give.

You have been regaled to-day with the heroic story of the rise and growth of your

Church. What a charming feast you have had! One of your own sons has painted with a master's hand, the pure and illustrious men who have been your Pastors. You have been reminded of your fathers and mothers, who lived in the service, and died in the embrace, of this Church. The deep voice of a century has spoken to you to-day, testifying to the faithfulness of God's word, and to the burning zeal of those who once constituted this Church. Can you resist these thrilling influences? Do they not inflame you with an ambition to attempt great things? If you can be stirred to noble deeds, it must be now. If these glories and festivities cannot lift you to great deeds, then you must die without knowing what it is to be noble. Standing in the line which parts the centuries and enriched by what the past has done for you, say what you will do for the future!

Remember, that you are committed. You are advertised for a great performance to-night. There is no escape for you. Your programme pledges you for a great act. Fail, and the world will laugh at your disaster.

Here hangs the picture of the glorified Jeter. You put it here in token of your esteem and honor. You are to lead the Virginia Baptists to-night in a movement to embalm his name. Do you work well; act in a manner worthy of the hour and the man, or else strike down his picture, and let him be forgotten.

THE CHURCH IN ITS RELATION TO MISSIONS.

BY

H. A. TUPPER.

THE CHURCH IN ITS RELATION TO MISSIONS.

THE missionary history of this Church divides itself into three periods of some thirty-three years each: *First*, from its organization in 1780 to 1813, when the "Foreign Missionary Society of Virginia" was formed in this Church; *Second*, from 1813 to 1846, when the Southern Baptist Convention held its first anniversary in this house; *Third*, from 1846 to 1880, when this Centenary of the Church—missionary in all its career—is celebrated.

FIRST PERIOD: FROM 1780 TO 1813.

That was missionary discipline when those fourteen members of the Boar Swamp Church went forth, in 1780, and constituted this Church in Franklin's house, on Union Hill; and further missionary experience when they set out again and erected their humble house of worship on Cary Street; and still missionary progress was it when they established themselves in the brick edifice, on the corner of Broad and College Streets; but the most missionary feature of these movements was the removal of Joshua Morris from Boar Swamp to Richmond, to labor for the infant Church, according to the historian Benedict, "at his own costs." Dr. Wm. D. Thomas says of Morris: "Surely the memory of this grand old pioneer missionary and planter of evergreen churches deserves to be cherished by the child of his youth." And how God blessed this missionary zeal of Church and Pastor is indicated in the fact that in 1808 the Church had grown from fourteen souls to five hundred and sixty, with several licensed preachers.

This Church was a prominent member of the Dover Association, constituted in 1783, which, like other Baptist Associations, was only a missionary body. Semple, in his "History of Virginia Baptists," published in 1810, says: "The chief business of these Associations was to receive petitions and appoint preachers to travel into new places where the gospel was likely to flourish." The formation itself of such Associations was an evidence of decided missionary spirit, inasmuch as it was done in spite of Baptist jealousy of church-independence; which jealousy was intensified by hatred to the hierarchal domination which had just been overthrown. The blessedness of the gospel sent to the destitute is described in an early Circular Letter of the Dover Association, in the language of Solomon: "As cold water to a thirsty soul, so is good news from a far country." A far country was Georgia, where our missionaries went—as far then as Asia is now. The biographer of one of these Evangelists speaks of his longing to preach the gospel in that "distant land," as he calls the South; and of his preaching in "various benighted regions;" and how this missionary spirit was still honored of the Lord appears in the statement of G. B. Taylor, that, in 1773, there were three thousand Baptists in Virginia; and of Benedict, that in 1812 there were thirty-five thousand. This is the more remarkable, as the first period of our Church's history started and ended in wars with Great Britain. Immediately after the "Old Revolution" the churches were in a sluggish spiritual state; but missionaries were active, and the churches stirred themselves, and God poured out copious blessings, from the mountains to the seaboard—reminding the aged people, doubtless, of the tidal waves of salvation that rolled over the land under the preaching of that foreign missionary, George Whitefield, and of the home missionaries, Stearns and Marshall and Harris, and others. Nor was the missionary intelligence and sympathy of our fathers less broad and deep than ours. Robert B. Semple—who was President of the Baptist Convention of Virginia, organized in this Church—and men of his stamp were warm and able advocates of foreign missions. Abraham Marshall, in his sketch of his father, Daniel Marshall, published in 1802, refers thus to the evangelization of the heathen: "The Scriptures have been translated into several barbarous languages. Missionaries have gone out literally into all the world, and sinners of all descriptions have fallen by thousands beneath the sword of the Spirit, which is the word of God."

The interest that John Courtney, the second Pastor of the Church, experienced in this subject may be inferred from his own missionary spirit, which possessed him to the very end. "Even when too old and infirm to dismount from his horse," says Dr. Burrows, "he rode, cane in hand, from door to door, and calling the friends out to him, would encourage, counsel, and exhort them, sometimes closing his interview with prayer on horseback in the street." This interest is also implied in the tribute voted to him in this Church by the Baptist Convention of Virginia, organized with special reference to Foreign Missions:—

"*Resolved, unanimously,* That this Convention cherish an affectionate remembrance of their lately deceased brother, Elder John Courtney, whose praise, as a laborer in the work of the Lord, is in all the churches. He has come to his grave as a shock of corn fully ripe."

The Church was ready for the visit of the returned missionary, Luther Rice, and the "Foreign Missionary Society of Virginia" was organized here in 1813—the year before the organization of the Triennial Convention. The testimony is indubitable that this Society was organized in 1813. At the Semi-Centennial "Jubilee" of the American Baptist Missionary Union, held in Philadelphia in 1864, Deacon William Crane, who was a member of this Church from 1812 to 1821, said that he assisted to organize this Society "in November, 1813." He was one of its original managers. J. B. Taylor, in his "Virginia Baptist Ministers," states that Samuel L. Straughan was sent by this Society as their missionary to Maryland, in 1814. But the point is put beyond all question.

The Fortieth Annual Report of the Society, made in 1853, opens with these words: "Forty years have passed,' that is from 1813, "since this Society came into existence. It was founded shortly after the return from India of our esteemed Brother Rice, and was among the first of those organizations which were represented in the Triennial Convention." Thus had this Church the honor of the organization, under its auspices, of the first Missionary Society of the South. William Crane said, " Perhaps south of Philadelphia."

The only remark I make on this first period of the Church's missionary history is that, being thus early called of God to the work of missions, the Church should manifest its appreciation of the honor, and its realization of its responsibility, by its perseverance and progress to the end. "The path of the just is as the shining light that shineth more and more unto the perfect day."

SECOND PERIOD: FROM 1813 TO 1846.
LUTHER RICE.

It would be strange if the enthusiasm on Foreign Missions, which was kindled by the return to this country of Luther Rice, and which swept like a sea of fire from Maine to Georgia, had not inflamed the First Baptist Church of Richmond. This place Mr. Rice called one of his three "homes;" and a home indeed did he find here under the hospitable roof of Archibald Thomas, and in the heart of the whole Church, whose funds were sometimes represented in the General Convention by this most eloquent advocate for the world's evangelization that America has ever produced.

THE FEMALE MISSIONARY SOCIETY.

On the last Sunday in March, 1817, Luther Rice preached the Anniversary Sermon of this Society. It must have existed at least a year before. The probabilities of its formation not long subsequent to Mr. Rice's first visit to Richmond, in 1813, is suggested by the fact, that, between 1816 and 1817, the Society was so strong that it contributed to Foreign Missions some five hundred dollars—only eighty or ninety of which was given under the persuasive eloquence of Mr. Rice's discourse.

Mrs. Archibald Thomas, lately fallen on sleep, was one of the early Treasurers of the Society.

In 1834, it was commended to the Dover Association by the Church as "increasing in efforts."

In 1836, it sent a delegate to the General Convention, having raised the year previous $314.83—of which $138.74 was for the outfit of the missionaries Shuck and Davenport. The next year, the Society gave $272.66; and in 1838, $418.89.

In 1846, the Society organized under the Southern Baptist Convention, and adopted as their missionary the Chinese convert, *Yong Seen Sang*, who was in this country with J. L. Shuck, and addressed the Society on the occasion. Since that day, this man of God, than whom there is no nobler Chinaman on our planet, has been sustained by this Society, as one greater than he was supported by honorable women of his day.

In thirty-eight years, the Society donated $6550. If the annual average, $172, be applied to the sixty-five years of its existence, the contributions of the Society to Foreign Missions will aggregate $11,180.

To avoid further reference to this Society, its officers, since its organization under the Southern Baptist Convention, may be here recorded:

Presidents: Mrs. Josephine Ryland, Mrs. Edward Kingsford, Mrs. Matilda Walthall, Mrs. A. G. Wortham, Mrs. Martha A. Page, Mrs. H. A. Tupper.

Vice-Presidents: Mrs. J. L. Burrows, Mrs. James Thomas, Jr.

Treasurer: Mrs. Archibald Thomas, Miss S. Pearce, Mrs. Coleman Wortham.

Secretaries: Miss Jane Reins, Miss S. Ligon, Mrs. Callie T. Ryland, Mrs. C. T. Knight.

Three of these ladies died while in office—Mrs. Josephine Ryland, Mrs. Callie T. Ryland, and Mrs. J. L. Burrows. Their memory is embalmed by the Society in touching and beautiful tributes.

RICHMOND AFRICAN BAPTIST MISSIONARY SOCIETY.

In his Memoir of James C. Crane, Dr. Burrows says of this man of God: "He was especially interested in the Mission to Africa. Mainly through the influence of his brother and himself, Lott Carey and Colin Teage, the first Baptist missionaries from America to Africa, were encouraged, equipped, and designated to that important field in 1821. To aid in the support of this mission, a Society had been organized in 1815, among the colored members of the Richmond churches, of which Society J. C. Crane was, for many years, the Secretary, corresponding with the missionaries abroad, and communicating with their supporters at home. This humble Society he loved to represent in public Anniversaries, Associations, and Conventions. He was their special delegate in the Triennial Convention of 1832, held in the city of New York. He continued the earnest friend and liberal supporter of African Missions and African Colonization, to the close of his life."

In a letter before me, dated "Richmond, February 22d, 1855," William Crane, senior brother of James C. Crane, writes: "In looking at the original Record Book of the Richmond African Baptist Missionary Society I find in the hand-writing of Lott Cary * * that it was formed the 26th of April, 1815. * * On Easter Monday, 1817, officers were elected—Wm. Crane, President, Colin Teage, Vice-President. * * I was, during the years 1815, '16, '17, and '18, engaged, for the benefit of the leading colored members of the Church, in a gratuitous school at the old Baptist Meeting House, * * at first in connection with Brother David Roper, * * and subsequently with Rev. John Bryce, Co-pastor of the Church. This African Missionary Society collected near one hundred dollars per annum, * * and seven hundred dollars were expended on the outfit of Lott Cary and Colin Teage." William Crane states also, that for fifteen or twenty years he was President or Secretary of this Society.

This work of these Crane brothers was honor enough for any two men ; and no little honor was it to this Church, of which they were members.

THE SEWING CIRCLE.

This Society is classed in this period, as it appears to be the successor of a venerable Society, to which an aged and former member of this Church makes in writing the following reference : " I think it was about this time that Mr. Luther Rice made his advent in Richmond. The Church was stirred to its depths. * * The proceeds of the Sewing Society were devoted to Foreign Missions, and the old ladies were constantly employed in knitting socks for the missionaries in Burmah." The ladies of the present Society will not object to link their history with that of the " Sewing Society " of these noble mothers in Israel, although the organization or re-organization of the " Sewing Circle" belongs strictly to a later period. Their official statement is as follows:

> The Sewing Society was organized November 30, 1855. Its object, to provide means for supporting a city missionary.
>
> Among its principal officers are the names of Mrs. J. L. Burrows, Mrs. James Thomas, Mrs. Edwin Wortham, Presidents; Mrs. C. Walthall, Mrs. E. W. Warren, and Mrs. J. B. Hawthorne, Vice Presidents; Mrs. Wilson Thomas, Mrs. Henry Hudnall, and Mrs. Lewis Frayser, Treasurers; Miss Mary Ella Thomas, Mrs. Samuel Harvey, and Miss Sallie Brockenbrough, Secretaries.
>
> Prior to the war we paid a city missionary from six to seven hundred dollars annually. For the past eight years we have assisted in the support of the Pastor of Venable-Street Church, paying now to that cause two hundred dollars annually. In addition to this we make contributions for the clothing of the Dorcas children.

Honorable mention must be made of Mrs. Martha A. Page, who is still with us, and of Mrs. M. E. Hillyard, who has crossed the river.

It should be added that the city missionary referred to above was I. T. Wallace, under whose valuable labors the "Fulton Section" was organized, which has grown into the Fulton Church of this city.

In the early part of the second period there was a "Judson Female Missionary Society," for the translation of the Scriptures into Burmese.

In 1823, Mrs. Ann Haseltine Judson wrote to the Society and thanked them for a contribution. Whether this was a distinct Society, or another form of the Sewing Society or of the Female Missionary Society, cannot be now ascertained. It is sufficient that the women of the Church, from these early dates, have been earnestly and variously engaged for the world's evangelization.

CHURCHES FOUNDED.

Reference has been made to the Fulton Church. Sidney was also "a section" of this Church. The Venable-Street Church sprang from a Sunday-school, under the conduct of our brother, Lewis Frayser. The Fourth Church was organized, in part, by members of this Church, and one of its pastors, Duncan R. Campbell, was of this Church. In 1820, members of this Church constituted the Second Church, which, for missionary discipline and energy, is second to none in the State. In 1854, the Leigh-Street Church was organized, mainly by members of the First Church, and now it is one of the largest white churches in the city.

In 1845, the First African Church, which is one of the three largest churches of the world, came out of ours. What centers of missionary influence have these churches become! What abundant fruit has been borne by these children of the old missionary Mother Church!

BAPTIST GENERAL ASSOCIATION OF VIRGINIA.

George B. Taylor, in his "Virginia Baptists," says: "In 1862, at the First Baptist Church, Richmond, the Constitution of the General Association was reported, and in 1823 it was adopted, and the body was organized under it." Henry K. Ellyson, Corresponding Secretary of the Association, writes, May 21, 1880: "In reading just now the address of Rev. James Fife at our semi-centennial, I notice that he refers to Rev. John Bryce as Pastor of the First Church in 1823. If he was, *he* must be put down as one of the founders of the General Association from your Church, being one of the delegates of 1823." From the file of the Richmond *Enquirer* of 1822, we find that the ministers in Richmond at that time were: John Buchanan, Richard Channing Moore, John Courtney, John H. Rice, David Roper, John Bryce, Wm. H. Hart, Peyton Anderson, and Jesse H. Turner. Mr. Bryce became Co-pastor of the Church in 1810, and resigned finally in 1822. Mr. Ellyson also writes: "It is within my personal knowledge that during the past thirty-three years the First Church has been the largest contributor to the treasuries of the Boards of the General Association and of the societies which were merged into the Association in 1855." Thus identified with the missionary work of the General Association, the First Church claims the privilege of recording the following statistics of the Association, from 1847 to 1880, furnished by the courtesy of its Corresponding Secretary: "In the past thirty-three years, we have had from fifteen to seventy-two missionaries in the field each year, averaging forty a year during all that time, not counting the four years of the war, when our work was suspended. During that time, 35,383 persons professed faith in Christ under their ministry; 223 churches and 487 Sunday-schools were organized by them; and they built 132 houses of worship."

In 1832, the First Church reported to the Association a "Male Missionary Society," and at the same time the addition of six hundred members, suggesting again that missionary labors return in blessings on the laborers, which is strikingly exemplified in the history of this Church and of the General Association.

In 1839, the Church reported: "We continue to patronize liberally our benevolent institutions."

In 1841, the membership of the Church, white and colored, was 2670 souls.

In 1823, when the General Association began its missionary career, there were 40,000 Baptists in this State.

Since 1845, the State has dispensed for missions outside of itself $276,027.37, and now there are 202,735 Baptists in the Commonwealth.

The President of the Association, when this paper was written, June 1, 1880, was J. L. M. Curry, of this Church.

BAPTIST CONVENTION OF VIRGINIA.

On Saturday evening, the 25th of December, 1824, Rice, Staughton, Dagg, and other distinguished gentlemen, met at the house of D. Roper, of this city, to confer with regard to the organization of the above Convention, as an auxiliary of the "General Convention of the Baptist Denomination in the United States." An invitation to "all friendly to missions" was issued to meet on the following Monday at the "First Church," where the Constitution was presented and the Convention organized. The following officers were elected:

President—Robert B. Semple.
Vice-President—Henry Keeling.
Corresponding Secretary—David Roper.
Recording Secretary—George Roper.
Treasurer—Anthony R. Thornton.
Other Managers—Madison Walthall, Peter Nelson, George Woodfin, Luther Rice, John L. Dagg, J. B. Jeter, John B. Valentine.

A strong address, by R. B. Semple, was published to arouse interest specially in the objects of the Triennial Convention. It is worthy of note that the Societies to be ancillary to this Convention were called "Primary or Mite Societies."

VIRGINIA FOREIGN MISSIONARY SOCIETY.

As has been stated, this Society was organized here in 1813. It was an enlargement, as to objects, upon the General Association of 1771, and the General Meeting of Correspondence of 1800. For many years it was an earnest auxiliary of the Triennial Convention.

In 1829, the Church happens to record that it took a public collection for the Society, but this was a common thing; and in 1847 it sent twenty delegates to the Society. In 1842, the Society urges the churches to observe "the Monthly Concert of prayer," at which our Church used to collect monthly some thirty or forty dollars for missions; and expresses the hope that Virginia would some day give ten thousand dollars a year to Foreign Missions, and the country one hundred and fifty thousand. In 1876, Virginia gave about that sum, and the country gives annually more than twice the one hundred and fifty thousand. But let it be said to the special honor of this Society that it reiterated the sentiment which I hope this Church will never forget, that no amount of money, or any other means, would suffice without the gift of the Holy Ghost. "Not by might, nor power; but by my Spirit, saith the Lord." From 1835 to 1855, the proceedings of the Society were published with those of the General Association, which, in the latter year, incorporated Missionary Boards in its Constitution, and the Virginia Foreign Missionary Society passed out of existence. Here it may be recorded that since the extinction of this Society, viz.: from 1856 to 1880, the contributions of our Church through the Missionary Boards of the Association, have been as follows: Home Missions,

$2,359.27; State Missions, $7,333.62; Foreign Missions, $8,901.74; total, $18,594.63. This venerable Society did not expire, however, until it had given birth to an institution greater than itself. In 1844, after the Board of the Triennial Convention had formally announced that it could not send any slave-holder into a missionary field, this Society issued an address, prepared by the then Pastor of this Church, J. B. Jeter, calling upon the churches of the South to meet in Convention to consider their duty under the circumstances. This was the origin of the Southern Baptist Convention, which was organized in Augusta, Ga., in May, 1845.

It should be added that members of this Church, as Archibald Thomas, James Sizer, and Christopher Walthall, were prominent officers of the Virginia Foreign Missionary Society, through many years of its honorable career. This Society should be "marked with a white stone."

TRIENNIAL CONVENTION AND SOUTHERN BAPTIST CONVENTION.

From 1813 to 1845, the missionary contributions of the Church and its societies went more or less directly to the Triennial Convention.

These contributions aggregated some $24,-680.82, which was about one-ninth of the sum, viz.: $215,856.26, given by the South for missions. But this Church gave also to the Convention the wise counsels of such gifted and godly men as James C. Crane and Jeremiah B. Jeter, who were ever enthusiastic advocates of missions. Yet, further, the Church contributed several of her noble sons, as Eli Ball and Robert Davenport and Samuel C. Clopton, to the foreign fields. Other missionaries were set apart here, and went forth with the prayerful blessing of this Church upon them, which blessing returned to the Church in the deepening and widening of its own missionary character.

After 1845, the missionary energy and contributions of the Church found a medium of communication with the fields of missions in the Southern Baptist Convention. Among the organizers of this Convention were these members of this Church: J. B. Jeter, E. Ball, H. Keeling, A. Thomas, J. C. Crane. Dr. Jeter was made President of the Board of Foreign Missions, which position he held for more than twenty years, and E. Ball, Vice President for Virginia. Archibald Thomas held the office of

Treasurer from the origin of the Convention until his death, and was succeeded by Edwin Wortham and John C. Williams. Charles T. Wortham was Auditor from 1845 to 1874. Of the original members of the Board, in addition to those mentioned, the following were from this Church: A. B. Smith, R. Ryland, A. G. Wortham, H. Keeling, J. Thomas, Jr., W. H. Gwathmey, and J. Talman, Sr. Thus was started in existence, by the pen of a Pastor of this Church, the Southern Baptist Convention, which has raised more than a million and a half of dollars for missions; has preached the gospel in dark places of the South and Southwest, and to the Indians and Chinamen of our country; while it has maintained missions in every continent of our globe, and been the instrument in God's hand of inducting thousands, if not tens of thousands, into the kingdom of heaven.

In reviewing this second period, " we thank God and take courage."

THIRD PERIOD: 1846 TO 1880.

The relation of the Church to missions, in this period, may be briefly stated:

I. ITS RELATION TO CITY, STATE, AND HOME MISSIONS.

Young Men's Missionary Society.

This Society was organized May 1, 1870. Its benevolence has extended to indigent children and college students; to State and Foreign Missions; and specially to a German Mission in the city. The amount contributed to these objects in ten years is $4,141.93. In 1878, J. B. Walthall, Chairman of the Prayer Meeting Committee of the Society, started a prayer meeting in connection with the "Shockoe Mission" on Fourth Street, between Jackson and Duval Streets. Ashton Starke and J. B. Walthall have successively superintended the mission since that time. A chapel was erected for the mission by J. H. Sands, of our Church. The mission is now divided—one part worshipping in the chapel, and the other in a hired room. The officers have been:

Presidents: C. McCarthy, J. B. Hill, F. Tupper, R. B. Lee.

Treasurer: H. M. Walthall.

Corresponding Secretaries: R. B. Lee, H. H. Watkins, R. S. Bosher, R. F. Patterson.

Recording Secretaries: C. E. Lacy, H. Bodeker, R. B. Lee, R. L. Woodward, P. Y. Tupper, F. W. Reins.

In 1833, a "Youth's Missionary Society" is reported to the Dover Association. In 1834, it was said to be making "increasing efforts." In 1836, it was represented in the General Association by our no longer youthful brethren, J. L. Apperson and Christopher Walthall. It is not held that this Society and the Young Men's Missionary Society are connected, except in respect to the class of persons, and to the similarity of the names and objects of the two societies.

Dorcas Society.

This Society was organized in 1868. One who is deeply interested in the organization furnishes the following statement of the object and results of the Society:

> The object of the Dorcas Society is to reach poor, ignorant, and outcast children; to clothe them, and bring them into the Sunday-school, and thus to put them under the influence of the gospel. As to the results of our work, God has allowed us to see the fruit of our labor. We have seen the idle and the vicious reclaimed; houses dark with poverty and intemperance lighted up with the beauty and the joy of the gospel; and the minds of children so moulded and guided as to give promise of abundant usefulness.

The officers of this Society are the same as

those of the "Sewing Circle;" but the management of the Society is committed to Mrs. Laura Rutherford, whom the writer of the above calls "our efficient officer." Associated with Mrs. Rutherford in this Christly work, are Mrs. Josiah Ryland, Miss N. L. Hill, and Miss Jane Stanard.

The Girls' Aid Society.

I cannot afford to add to, or take from, the following report from the President of this Society, a single word:

> The Girls' Aid Society was organized January 30, 1880, in the side chapel of the First Baptist Church. The meeting was called to order and the officers elected. Miss America A. Johnson was chosen President; Miss Katie Jude, First Vice-President; Miss Willie Callaham, Second Vice-President; Miss Georgia Burress, Secretary; Miss Mary Sweeney, Treasurer. The Society has raised $17.35; of which ten dollars has been given to aid the Dorcas children. So far, the expenses have been only one dollar and a half, ninety cents of which was spent to buy a basket to put the fancy work in, and the remaining sixty cents was spent for Record and Account Books. Dues are paid to the amount of five cents a month. The Society was organized with thirteen members, and now has a membership of forty-one.

May the Society live a hundred years!

2. THE CHURCH'S RELATION TO FOREIGN MISSIONS.

The Sunday-school.

Mrs. M. F. Dabney says, that in the earliest

days of the school, there was a "Cent Society," and each scholar was required to give a penny a week to the heathen. I may venture on high authority to say, that in the past ten or fifteen years the school has averaged some one hundred dollars per annum for missions. The Infant Class has contributed in ten years at least five hundred dollars. With such seed-corn what a harvest of missionary beneficence may be hoped for in the future of the Church!

Missionary Society of Richmond Female Institute.

In 1856, a Deacon of this Church, full of the spirit of Missions, gave, with his sister, $1,000 to found a Missionary Society for the young ladies of this Institution. A letter to this Society from our Missionary, Mrs. T. P. Crawford, was probably the means, under God, of leading Miss Edmonia Moon to China. Thence, perhaps, Miss Lottie Moon; and thence, what endless consequences of good! May the Society revive, and long live, and send other distinguished representatives to their perishing sisters of pagan lands!

Central Committee of Southern Baptist Convention, and Mite Box Committee of Woman's Missionary Society of Richmond.

This Central Committee was appointed by the Board of Foreign Missions, agreeably to an action of the Southern Baptist Convention, in 1878. Mrs. Edwin Wortham, of this Church, is the Corresponding Secretary. Some thirty or forty societies have been organized in the State, under the auspices of the Committee. This Committee is identified with the Woman's Missionary Society of Richmond, of which Mrs. J. B. Jeter has been the only President. This Society was organized, April 4th, 1872, for the support of Miss Edmonia Moon. "Committees on Mite Boxes" were appointed for the several Baptist Churches of the city. Mrs. John A. Belvin was the first Chairman of the Committee for the First Church. Mrs. H. A. Tupper is the present Chairman. The Committee has raised $1,396.40. The first Vice-President of the Society was Mrs. J. L. Burrows, whose decease was tenderly lamented by the Society. Mrs. H. A. Tupper succeeded to the office. Mrs. J. K. Connally of this Church, was the first Corresponding Secretary; and Mrs. J. Temple has been the only Treasurer. Besides the support of Miss E. Moon, the Society donated $700 for the house of Miss L. Moon. Recently it has contributed to the support of Mrs. Crawford, of Tung Chow. The handsome amount raised by the Society is $5,405.57.

Young Ladies' Missionary Society.

This Society was formed, May 20th, 1875, as a sewing society. Its first object was City Missions. Aid was afforded to the Venable Street Church. Subsequently its energies were directed to State Missions. A. Bagby, of West Point, and G. Gray, of Craig County, were assisted. November 12th, 1878, Miss Sallie Stein, missionary to China, was adopted by the Society, at a salary of five hundred dollars per annum. Before her departure from this country, the Society advanced to her $355.94. It is proper to state that a missionary society of the Macon, (Ga.,) Baptist Church, of which our former Pastor, E. W. Warren, is the pastor, has contributed fifty dollars to the treasury of this Society. The officers have been as follows:

Presidents—Miss Nettie Pleasants, Miss Sic Pleasants, Miss Sallie Knight, Miss Lelia Berry.

Vice-Presidents—Miss Sic Pleasants, Kate McCurdy, Lelia Berry, Mary T. Wortham, Ida Hill, Annie G. Tupper.

Treasurers—Mrs. D. O. Davis, Mrs. E. J. Bosher, Mrs. Furman Tupper.

Secretaries—Misses Sophie Bosher and Sallie Hundley.

The amount raised by the Society in five years is some twelve hundred dollars. The Board of Foreign Missions reported to the Southern Baptist Convention, at its past meeting, that the action of this Society was "heroic."

Rooms, Officers, Advocates.

1. The rooms of the Board of Foreign Missions were in this house for more than twenty-five years.

2. All the Presidents of that Board, except one, and all of its Treasurers, have been of this Church. The Recording Secretary, a Deacon of this Church, has held his office since 1851, and is the only surviving member of the original managers now on the Board. The Corresponding Secretary, who has just published a history of the "Foreign Missions of the Southern Baptist Convention," is a member of this Church. With three exceptions, every officer of the

Board, from its origin to the present, has been of this Church.

3. Need I say that the Church has numbered among its membership some of the warmest friends and ablest advocates of Foreign Missions?

I have referred to Archibald Thomas, James C. Crane, James Thomas, Jr., and others not of the ministry. Time would fail me to enumerate the many more of this class. I have also referred, among the Pastors, to Joshua Morris, John Courtney, and John Bryce. Only a word with regard to the others. Andrew Broaddus preached every Annual, or Sunday Sermon, of the Dover Association when present, from 1797 to 1843, and significant was his specifying men of such renowned missionary character in an exclamation of his valedictory address to the Rappahannock: "Where are Straughan, and Semple, the brother of my soul, and Luther Rice? Where are they?" Henry Keeling was first Vice President of that Foreign Mission body, the Baptist Convention of Virginia, and was one of the founders of the Southern Baptist Convention. John Kerr, described by Dr. Jeter as "vigorous in his efforts" for missions, was chosen, in 1836, by the Baptist Convention of North Carolina, as the most suitable men to preach the funeral sermon of that apostle of modern missions, Luther Rice. Of Isaac T. Hinton, Dr. Burrows says: "Under his pastorate here, various societies for missionary and benevolent purposes were formed;" and J. B. Taylor, "whose life was missions," says he was most faithful in proclaiming salvation "to destitute churches," and in the then missionary field of New Orleans, he was in his zeal, "self-sacrificing and consuming." J. B. Jeter was the soul of our missionary boards, and may be called *the Father of the Southern Baptist Convention.* What shall I say of Pastors Manly and Burrows and Warren? There are no truer friends and abler advocates of this cause, as may be said also of the present pastor, J. B. Hawthorne, and our absent brother, the President of the Foreign Mission Board, J. L. M. Curry.

At the close of this period, we may set up our Ebenezer, saying, "Hitherto hath the Lord helped us."

SUMMARY.

The Church, including Societies and Sunday-school, gives annually to missions some thirty-two hundred dollars. From 1813 to 1880 the contributions for this cause, so far as they appear in various records and can be estimated, aggregate some $60,310.61. But the moral influence of the Church, in favor of spreading the gospel, has been far greater than its monetary power. Born not only from above, but amid the throes of the human mind, which brought forth the three great forces of modern civilization, viz.: government guaranteeing civil and religious liberty; the Sunday-school institution; and the present enterprise of Foreign Missions—the Church was expected to embody no little of that aggressiveness which is a prime factor in the progress of the nineteenth century. The expectation has not been disappointed. The Church has kept abreast of the missionary spirit of the age, in its long race of one hundred years. But, " Not unto us, O Lord, not unto us; but unto thy name give glory, for thy mercy and thy truth's sake."

WHAT OF THE FUTURE?

At the next Centennial Celebration of this Church, Foreign Missions will, in all probability, be a thing of the past. Our Home Field will then be commensurate with our planet. But before this consummation, much labor must be performed. At the present rate of our contributions, some three thousand dollars per annum, our contribution to the world's redemption in the one hundred years would be three hundred thousand dollars.

Dr. John A. Broadus says the Baptists of the South should give this year to missions a million of dollars. What is our proportion? What should be our aggregate reported at the next centenary gathering? "Wherefore, seeing we also are compassed about with so great a cloud of witnesses, let us lay aside every weight, and the sin that doth so easily beset us, and let us run with patience the race that is set before us, looking unto Jesus, the author and finisher of our faith."

Let our unceasing prayer be: "Lord, increase our faith; Lord, grant thy Holy Spirit." And in the day of final accounts, may it be said of The Old First Baptist Church of Richmond, with regard to the execution of the great commission to God's people: "SHE HATH DONE WHAT SHE COULD."

ORIGIN AND HISTORY

OF

THE FIRST AFRICAN CHURCH.

BY

ROBERT RYLAND.

FIRST AFRICAN CHURCH.

ABOUT the year 1838 the First Baptist Church of Richmond, then under the pastoral care of Rev. J. B. Jeter, determined, after mature consultation, to build the house of worship, which they now occupy, on the corner of Broad and Twelfth Streets. To this they were urged by several motives. Their old house was becoming too small for the congregation. It was not situated in an eligible place. Its architecture, long the sport of its neighbors, was far behind the times. The mixed character of the audience, composed of white and colored people, was thought to militate seriously against the progress of the Church. The colored element was so large, that only a small part of it could be furnished with sittings. Its spiritual oversight was still more difficult to be managed. A large proportion of this class, being slaves, could not be reached and disciplined, except by persons of their own color. Few of them could attend the church-meetings. And the instructions of the pulpit could not be always adapted especially to their wants. It was quite evident, also, that the new edifice could not be so designed, either in size or structure, as to admit the mixed congregation, with any convenience to either class. The interests of both, therefore, imperatively demanded their permanent separation. But how could this be effected? Could the Church afford to *give up* the old house and lot to the blacks, at the very time that she was erecting a new house on a new lot at a cost of some forty thousand dollars? If she should conclude to relinquish half the appraised value of the old property to the colored brotherhood, would they be able and willing to pay for the other half, at a time when they were just assuming the expenses of separate worship? Questions still more grave and delicate were yet to be solved. Would the law of the State allow a distinct organization for *colored* worshippers? And if the measure were strictly legal, would *public sentiment*, on some subjects far more potent and more jealous than law, quietly acquiesce in the arrangement?

These were the preliminary points that had to be adjusted before any decisive plans could be matured. They all required a clear head and a steady hand. And such were the head and hand of the Pastor. His prominent coadjutors were Richard C. Wortham, James Sizer, Richard Reins, Samuel Hardgrove, and Archibald and James Thomas, all but one of whom have gone to their final reward. It was first ascertained, by consulting able jurists, that the law allowed colored persons to be organized for separate worship, provided a *white minister* should always conduct the worship. On this point, public sentiment was somewhat divided. Some persons were strongly opposed to the measure. Others were coldly in favor of it, but a large majority were indifferent, or at least not disposed to express any opinion, till they could see how the plan would work. The First Church determined to allay prejudice and to guard against danger by appointing a Committee of eighteen discreet brethren to act as supervisors of the African Church. Of this committee, twelve were from the First, four from the Second, and two from the Third, now Grace Street, Church. These were to elect the Pastor, and two of them were to be present with him at all the gatherings for public worship. Like all other Committees, this was more easily appointed, than it was induced to attend to the duties prescribed. It is but just, however, to add that some of the appointees, especially of the First Church, did attend regularly, in their turn, at all the meetings of the African Church on the Lord's Day.

The pecuniary questions were not so hard to settle. It was decided to have the property appraised and to have it deeded to the colored people, as soon as they should pay rather more than half its estimated value. It was assessed at $13,500. One of the brethren of the First Church, well skilled both in giving and in urging others to give, agreed to collect three thousand dollars of this fund from leading citizens of Richmond, outside of Baptist circles. And the colored brethren were informed that they could occupy the old house, as soon as it should be vacated by the whites, and that, on their payment of the remaining forty-five hundred dollars, which they thought they could raise, the property should be deeded to Trustees, to be held by them for the *exclusive and perpetual use* of the First African Baptist Church. Both these pledges were redeemed, and in the year

1849 the property was conveyed to its present incumbents, who had paid $5,000.19, principal and interest.

Dr. Jeter drew up the Constitution of the African Church. It was more Presbyterial than congregational in its features. It provided for the selection of thirty Deacons from the colored members, and of a white Pastor, by the Supervising Committee, subject, however, to the approval of the whole colored membership. This Board of Deacons, in which vacancies were to be filled by a popular vote, was to be, in conjunction with the Pastor, the permanent ruling power in the body. But should its decisions be unsatisfactory to a certain number of its constituents, provision was made for an appeal to the Supervising Committee. Only twice was such an appeal ever taken. The salary of the Pastor was fixed at five hundred dollars per annum, to be raised by penny collections at every meeting. But if these should prove inadequate, the three white Baptist churches assumed the responsibility of supplying the deficiency. They were never called on for any aid in this regard, simply because it was not needed.

The humble writer of this paper, then connected with the Richmond College, was chosen Pastor of the new organization. The motives that led him to accept the appointment were various: 1. He had been preaching every Lord's Day to country churches, but their remoteness was sometimes inconvenient, requiring his absence from home and College about two days of the week. 2. He felt that the separation of the two classes would remove a great impediment from the path of the First Church, and thus indirectly advance its prosperity in all coming time, and that *he* had no *right* to *excuse* himself from the duty of *helping forward* so important an object. 3. Since the passage of a law by the Virginia Legislature, forbidding all colored preachers to minister to their people in divine things, he felt that all the ministers of Christ, and especially those of his own denomination, were called on to put forth new efforts to evangelize the people of color. In fact, slavery, as it existed in all the Southern States, had long been a burden to his mind. Not that he believed it to be, *semper et ubique* a *sin*, but that some grievous sins were closely and constantly *connected* with it. The separation of husbands and wives, and of parents and young children, for mere gain, and the prohibition to teach colored children to read the word of God, except under very limited conditions, he regarded as *glaring wrongs*. He had always seen in slavery, however, the mysterious hand of God leading the African to Jesus, and thus making the wrath of man to praise him. But that negroes, without exception, should be forbidden to preach, however qualified and sanctioned by their respective churches, *this* seemed not only to violate freedom of conscience in regard both to the whites and the blacks, but to attempt to contravene the manifest purpose of God in permitting the institution of slavery. In common with all his thoughtful fellow-citizens, he had long been oppressed with these reflections, but the whole subject was too delicate and embarrassing to admit of ventilation. The Virginia pulpit has an instinctive aversion to the discussion of politico-religious subjects. And now that Providence had opened a way, for his personal efforts, to elevate an unfortunate race, and thus to mitigate, in some degree, their servitude, this was a real solace to his heart. 4. In addition to these inducements, he had long regarded the Christianization of the millions of Africa as likely to be brought to pass only by the conversion of the

Americo-African, and by his mission, with the true faith, to the land of his forefathers. If the gospel must be preached " to every creature," how could one, with the vows of Heaven upon him, refuse to enter so promising a field of usefulness? If it was his duty to aid the Foreign Mission Board, according to his humble measure, in sending the word of life to the heathen nations *abroad*, how could he decline to preach that word, at his own door, to a people, many of whom—not all—were practically heathen? These arguments were too weighty and far-reaching to be counterbalanced by the odium that would certainly be connected with the office of a "*nigger preacher.*" He entered this field on the first Sunday in October, 1841, and was cordially received by the whole congregation. The revised list of actual members contained about one thousand. The thirty Deacons, who constituted the ruling element of the Church, were an intelligent, godly, and highly respected body of men. He verily believes that, in all their religious convocations, they, each and every one, had at heart only their own spiritual culture, the salvation of their people, the peace and order of society, and the glory of God.

Having been often asked what course he

pursued in discharging his pastoral functions, he has always replied: "I treat the colored people from the pulpit, and in all my presidings as Moderator, and in all my official intercourse, exactly as I would a white congregation, *i. e.*: with the *greatest possible respect.*" If they were slaves, he thought of them as Christ's freemen, —if free, as Christ's slaves. In truth, brethren, the gospel knows no white, no black, no rich, no poor, no bond, no free, no North, no South, no East, no West. The gospel was devised for man, and man needs the gospel.

There were, however, some strongly marked peculiarities in the congregation, to which the Pastor, of course, aimed to adapt his teachings. He sought to be instructive, rather than pathetic—to dwell on the distinctive doctrines and precepts of Christianity, rather than on its metaphysical refinements—to preach *out* of their minds their dreams and fancies, their visions and revelations, and all their long cherished superstitions—and to preach *into* their minds a knowledge of the great facts of their religion, with its consequent doctrines, obligations, and privileges. That this mode of teaching was not wholly ineffectual was shown by the two following representative cases:

An intelligent-looking man, whose name I did not know, came to me at the close of a meeting one day, and said, with evident concern: "Brother Ryland, you've preached away nearly all my religion. What is left is hanging by a single thread." "What is that thread?" I inquired. "Jesus Christ died to save sinners. They must trust alone in him," he answered. "Well, that thread," said I, with a smile, "is strong enough to hold you up."

A lad, about twelve years of age, was presenting himself as a candidate for baptism. Among other questions, I asked him *why* he wished to be baptized. "In Mark xvi. 16," he replied, "Jesus says, 'He that believeth and is baptized shall be saved.' I believe in him, and now I wish to obey his command."

Especially did the Pastor labor, with all the plainness and point which our language affords, to impress on them the law of chastity. This he regarded as their great necessity, and he had reliable testimony from themselves that a great revolution on this subject was wrought among them during the years of his ministry with them.

He wrote a Catechism, of fifty-two lessons, for the benefit of the entire congregation. The questions were so formed as to require the answer, "yes," or "no," and a passage of Scripture was then quoted to prove the answer. It is believed that much good resulted from memorizing at least one proof-text on the various topics introduced into the lessons.

It had long been the habit of many of the attendants to come late to meeting. This habit was not only hurtful to those who indulged it, but it disturbed the quietness of the audience and interrupted the preaching. At first, the pastor thought that the employers might have detained their house-servants so long, as to prevent their reaching the sanctuary in time. On inquiry, he found that most of the families, who permitted their servants to come at all, allowed them ample time to secure punctuality. He found, moreover, that when there was a marriage to be solemnized, or something amusing to be exhibited, everybody was in time. After trying by moral suasion, very urgently, but in vain for several years, to break up this annoyance, he induced the Deacons to pass an order that the church-yard gates should be locked forty-five minutes after the time to begin worship, so as to exclude incomers after the sermon began. This measure seemed harsh, but its effect was most salutary. Very few were really kept out, and loiterers were taught a valuable lesson. The evil being, to a great degree, corrected, the rule was, after six months, suspended.

During the last four or five years of his connection, the Pastor taught a Sunday-school for children and youth on Lord's Day morning. Although only *oral* instruction could be lawfully given, yet many valuable ideas were imparted to the four hundred attendants. Many beautiful hymns taught, and many striking portions of Scripture committed to memory, could not have failed of happy results.

There were several ministers of respectable gifts in the Church, who, at the request of private families and by the connivance of the officers of the law, often attended funerals in the city and the adjacent country. But it was thought to be the wisest and kindest course, to keep all the services at the Church strictly within the provisions of the law. These brethren, therefore, were never invited to occupy the pulpit. But, as a sort of recompense for this slight, they, and others, were called on to pray, several times, at each religious service. Many of these prayers exhibited great fervency and power, and afforded the highest degree of comfort, both to those who offered them and to those who heard them. The singing by the choir was performed with scientific skill and Christian heartiness, but when the vast congregation poured out its full soul in the old-fashioned songs, the long and loud bursts of praise reminded one of the "sound of many waters." There is no doubt but that to these devotional accompaniments—prayer and praise—was due the largest part of the spirituality of the Church, and of the success of the ministry in winning souls. A colored brother was never *known* to refuse to pray in public when called upon. He did the very best he was able to do, and the Master asks no more. "Who hath ears to hear, let him hear."

There were usually at our College some twenty or twenty-five young men, studying for the ministry. And, like theologians generally, most of them were not burdened with money. Partly to help their pockets and partly to improve their gifts, as well as to get assistance in his arduous work, the Pastor often invited these young men to officiate for him in the afternoon. At the close of a sermon by one of these, Deacon Simms, an excellent man, was requested to follow with prayer. He offered up a devout petition to God for his blessing on the truths just delivered, and for large grace "on our stripling young brother that is trying to learn how to preach."

The good order of the congregation was remarkable—for its size, it was *wonderful*. During the twenty-four years of his ministry among them, the Pastor did not see a single instance of a group of persons, young or old, engaged in talking and laughing during public worship.

The financial business was divided among several Committees, who, having collected the funds and distributed them to their appropriate objects, made to the Church quarterly reports of their respective doings. These reports were uniformly entered on the church records. The Pastor, who also acted as clerk, recollects no instance of a single report being not ready when called for, or having an error in the additions—or a conflict between the "balance in hand" at the close of one quarter and its entrance on the report for the next quarter. He believes that no defalcation occurred, or was even suspected, in the handling of these funds. His salary, with the exception of the first two years, when the training process was incomplete, was cheerfully and promptly paid at the close of every quarter. "Who hath ears to hear, let him hear."

In the year 1846, the Second African Church was constituted under the auspices of the Second Baptist Church. So far as my knowledge extends, this body has enjoyed a high degree of prosperity. One of its leading members once complained to me so bitterly of his pastor that it seemed *proper* to suggest that he should be requested to resign. "We have offered him his resignation," said he, "but he would not accept it."

About the year 1855, it was found to be necessary to send out a *colony* from the First African Church. Its number of members had grown to three thousand, and its house was quite inadequate to their accommodation. By the cordial assent and co-operation of the brotherhood, a lot was purchased in the neighborhood of Bacon Quarter Branch, and a neat edifice was built. It was dedicated the fifth Sunday in May, 1858, and the Ebenezer Church, consisting of four hundred members, was soon afterwards constituted. This property, which cost a little over eight thousand dollars, was paid for and deeded to Trustees for the benefit of the Church just before the close of the late war. These two churches—the mother and the daughter, have cherished mutual harmony in their efforts to advance the cause of God.

From October 1st, 1841, to July 1st, 1865, the additions by baptism to the First African Church were three thousand eight hundred and thirty-two. Of this number, no larger a proportion fell away from the belief and practice of the truth, than is usual in our average churches. It was thought best to discourage a *hasty profession of religion* among them. The applicants for admission were required to bring testimonials of good or improving characters. They were then examined by some Deacon or experienced member, and kindly admonished as to the responsibility about to be assumed. They were then brought before the Pastor, who satisfied himself in regard to their intelligence and their fitness for the new relation. Had the *persuasive*, instead of the *restraining*, policy been pursued, the number of the baptized might easily have been doubled. It seemed very important to impress especially the younger candidates with a deep sense of the fearful guilt of *trifling with their souls and with their God*.

In respect to the *popular* feeling of Richmond towards the Church, the Pastor takes leave to say that among the *highest circles* of society he believes there was the *kindest interest* felt in its welfare and permanence. To say that no suspicions were cherished—that no surmisings were expressed—that no diminution of respect and appreciation was shown by some persons, would be going beyond the limits of truth. It sometimes requires a little moral courage to obey the dictates of conscience. But let all this pass. Of the resident clergy of the city, Dr. Jeter excepted, no one evinced more sympathy with, and more regard for, the well-being of the Church than the late Bishop Johns. He often preached for us, and seemed quite gratified when, on one occasion, he was complimented as a "first-rate nigger preacher." All the annual meetings of the several denominations, when convened in the city, were invited to supply the pulpit, not only on Sundays, but on the secular days—and those sent preached with great acceptance, and expressed themselves as delighted with the order and decorum of the assembly.

At the close of the war, the constitution and rules of order were so far modified, as to adapt them to the new relations which the colored people sustained to society. The Pastor then offered his resignation, from a belief that they would *naturally* and *justly* prefer a minister of their own color. This resignation was proposed and accepted with mutual kindness and good will. It has always seemed incongruous that a Baptist minister should argue stoutly in behalf of the popular election of church-officers, and then complain if *he* is not chosen or continued in office.

A few general remarks will finish what I have to say.

It is a misconception of the African race, which many Anglo-Saxons cherish, *that all negroes are alike*. While the whole human family are depraved, and the sameness of condition, surrounding a particular tribe, will impress on it a peculiar type of character, still there is as much *individuality*—as much variety of intellectual and moral temperament—among the negroes as there is among persons of any other race. I have witnessed as bright examples of godliness, of disinterested kindness, of real gentility of manners, and of native mental shrewdness among them, as among other people. Many of the old men and matrons were brought up in the best families, and understood all the proprieties of life. Their manners were polished, and their principles correct. This, to a partial extent, was true of some of the young people of both sexes. Say you this was the result of imitation? Very well. And do not our children get all their refinement by imitation? Let me give you specimens of the traits just enumerated.

Nicholas Scott was an old man, whom some of the present citizens will remember. He was the owner and driver of a hack, and before the day of railroads, used to take John Marshall, William Wickham, B. Watkins Leigh, and other distinguished lawyers, to the court-houses in the adjoining counties. He was highly esteemed by them for his upright and obliging temper, and caught their dignified bearing and courtly manners. He had always something to say for their amusement, calling himself *Old Nick*. Having returned from the North, after a sojourn there of a year or two, he met one of these gentlemen on the street, and, after the mutual greetings, being asked why he had come back to Old Virginia, he said: "Oh, sir, the North is no place for a *gentleman*." I knew him only as a matured Christian. While he was hearing the gospel, his face was radiant with intelligence and joy. He came up to the College once to see me when sick, and brought me a little basket of eggs. I could not but notice the delicacy with which he offered his present, and the modesty and skill with which he administered the comforts of religion. I called to see him in his last illness. He was lying on a bed whose sheets, pillow-cases, and counterpane were marvelously white and clean, and in an humble chamber of corresponding neatness. He seemed perfectly rational, fully aware of his approaching end, and more than willing to depart. "I am all packed up and ready to start on my long journey," said he, alluding to his former mode of life; "but I don't want to go one moment sooner, or stay one moment longer, than the Master wills." Thus he died. And I witnessed many similar deaths among those people. "The Lord knoweth them that are his."

Aaron Lee was a coarser, rougher, more plebeian specimen of sable humanity. His master had such entire confidence in his honesty, that he used to send his checks by him to the bank for deposit. One day, Aaron reached the bank just after it was closed, and he had to hold his check till the next morning. Happening to be caught out that night by a policeman, after the lawful hour, he was lodged in the watch-house, and the next morning taken before the mayor. Being asked by his Honor, with some surprise, why *he* had been caught on the street without a "pass" at an unseasonable hour, he answered that he *had* a pass, but it was in the same pocket with a large check, and, as he did not know what sort of a man the officer was, he chose to go to the lock-up, rather than to pull out his pass and check together to be inspected by the officer.

The sexton of Dr. Jeter's Church was a member of the African Church. One Lord's Day afternoon, Dr. Jeter and I exchanged pulpits, and the sexton went down to his own congregation, expecting to hear me. After closing the exercises at the First Church, I walked down to see that the people were retiring quietly, and to ask if everything had gone on smoothly. Meeting with the young sexton, I inquired: "Who preached for you this afternoon?" "Dr. Jeter." "What was his text?" "The same he took at his own Church this morning"—repeating it. "Did he preach the same sermon?" "Just the same, except that he left out one paragraph addressed to the rich, because he thought we had no *rich people* down here."

One of my members went, on a certain occasion, to hear a learned gentleman, then a Pastor of this city. I do not vouch for the justice of the criticism, but, being asked how he liked the sermon, he said: "He preaches too much out of the dictionary."

A prominent preacher among his brethren was making an address at our communion, and said: "There was no death among the ancient people of God during the days of Moses. He made a brazen serpent and put it up on a high pole. And whosoever looked upon it was saved from death. And I reckon they all must have looked upon it, for Paul says 'death reigned from Adam to Moses.' And if he reigned from Adam *to* Moses, he could not have reigned after Moses came."

Sometimes I was called on to decide controversies on knotty points of interpretation. Two young men brought a disputed case about the five barley loaves, mentioned in the miracle of the loaves and fishes. One of them contended that the loaves were made of barley as we make bread of wheat and corn. The other, more given to abstruse speculation, maintained that the loaves were so *small* that they were *barely* loaves.

To vary the exercises, so as to take them out of the deep-worn ruts, I sometimes stood up in the pulpit and invited any one to interrogate me on points of doctrine that might be bearing on his mind. A brother rose up one Sunday and said: "Prophecy foretold that a bone of Christ should not be broken. Suppose the soldiers, who broke the legs of the two malefactors, had *tried* to break the legs of Christ, do you think *they could have done it?*" These are specimens of their mental processes, and which of you, learned divines, ever struck out thoughts of greater *originality* than these?

There was a spirit of inquiry among them. It came in my way, in one of my sermons, to state and expose some of the learned nonsense of Baron Swedenborg. The next day I happened in a book-store, and the merchant told me that the young man whom I met going out had just inquired for the works of Baron Swedenborg.

A sort of club among the young men of a certain section of the city met every Sunday night to talk over the sermons of the day. One was called on to give the text, another the divisions, a third the doctrine, duties, etc., of the discourse, until, by one or another, the whole sermon, if it was worth anything, was reproduced.

I often witnessed cases of disinterestedness that were really touching. Having spent the night with a gentleman in Hanover, during one of my vacation-trips in the interest of the College, I observed, next morning, that my horse was nicely combed and curried, and, as was usual in those days, I offered the boy a dime for his attention. He stepped back and said, with an air of the greatest kindness: "I couldn't possibly take anything from my *Pastor*." Indeed, that spirit pervaded the whole Church. As my salary had been fixed by the Superintending Committee, and as I was afraid they might feel oppressed by the sum, having other burdens to bear, I proposed, at the close of the second year, to the Board of Deacons, that they should reduce the sum to four hundred dollars, and requested them to have a separate meeting, and, after consulting the brethren generally, to decide and report by the next month. They resolved, unanimously, that the salary should not be reduced.

Strangers may ask how they raised the

means for all these church expenditures. I answer: 1. Many of them, being free, were good mechanics, waiters, and drivers, and received living wages. 2. The slaves had their food, clothing, lodging, and medical attendance from their masters, and whatever money they gathered up was for other purposes. 3. All the factory hands had "tasks" assigned to them, and, if they were expert and diligent, they always did "*overwork*," for which they were promptly paid. Some of them told me that they sometimes received on Saturday night more wages for themselves than they had earned for their masters. 4. *All* the slaves had perquisites of some kind. If called on to do extra work, or to serve at unusual times, or if they showed marked fidelity, they were generally recompensed. 5. My own servants, when we were about to furnish their fall or spring clothing, would often say that, by patching their old garments, they could do without *new* ones, and would ask us for the *money* instead. Of course, we had no objection to this plan, unless we suspected a vicious use of the money. I suppose other families pursued the same course. Thus the servants often bought the first shad, the first watermelon, the first strawberries, of the season, long before their masters could afford such luxuries for *their* tables. 6. Add to all this, I am happy to say, that some masters gave their servants money especially to meet their church expenses. Each attendant gave at least one cent at every meeting, and a congregation of a thousand, worshipping twice on the Lord's Day, will raise a thousand dollars a year without any conscious sacrifice.

And now, brethren, as I have perhaps detained you too long with these minute details, I will close with one remark. The negroes are now all free, and I am heartily glad of it, though I say nothing of the agencies and methods by which the event was accomplished. They are our fellow-*men*—our fellow-*citizens*— and many of them our fellow-*Christians*. Let us treat them in the spirit of our common Christianity. And let us remember that its *leading doctrine*, in respect to our relations to man, is: "*Love worketh no ill to his neighbor, therefore love is the fulfilling of the law.*"

FRATERNAL ADDRESSES

BY

BASIL MANLY,
E. W. WARREN,
H. McDONALD.

ADDRESS.

BY BASIL MANLY.

I WAS startled, the other day, to find how venerable I had become. I called to see our honorable sister, Miss Lucy Courtney, in her solitude of perfect deafness and entire blindness—bowed under the weight of fourscore and ten years. As soon she had spelled out my name by her system of signals, she startled me, not more by the affectionate embrace with which she honored me than by designating me as "Dear Brother Manly, the oldest living Pastor of the First Church." I had never thought of it before. Though younger in years than all my successors, except the present incumbent, I am left, by the death of Dr. Jeter, the Senior Surviving Pastor.

It is difficult for me to realize that it is about thirty years since I arrived in Richmond at the call of this Church, a youth of twenty-four, with no pastoral experience, except for a single year with country churches in Alabama, and in frail health. It seems to me as but yesterday, when the "young men" of this Church met me at the depot, Coleman Wortham, Robert Bosher and W. H. Gwathmey, and conducted me to the hospitable Wortham mansion on Grace Street, which ever afterwards felt like a home to me. A brief sojourn in the family of James C. Crane gave me a similar freedom of intercourse with that noble brother and his household. And then my more permanent abode was taken up with Brother Archibald Thomas, to whose warm heart, sound judgment, and honest, earnest energy, not only I, but this whole Church, owe so much.

How I lament that she, who survived him, and who was so long the light of his home, and the hospitable, cheerful, generous Mother in Israel, did not live to enjoy this day, and to receive the honors which grateful hearts would rejoice to render her—one of the noblest Christian women that I ever knew, a second mother to me.

I remember that just at the time of my arrival here, Rev. James B. Taylor was passing through that critical illness which threatened to deprive us of his valuable services. And every day for weeks I visited his house to inquire, and to offer my assistance in attending him. Thank God, many years of useful labor were granted to him, and of happy companionship to me.

I would gladly speak of the brethren who seemed to be pillars in those days—the Deacons; the Sunday School Superintendent, James Thomas; the younger active members; of D. R. Crane, with his cheering face and melodious voice; of Charles Wortham, the "eleventh hour laborer," as he modestly called himself—prominent and faithful, though gray-headed and infirm, in the young men's meeting; of many others, old and young, whose names and faces come freshly up to me; but time would not allow, and that duty has been appropriately assigned to others.

During the four years that I supplied this pulpit, I may truly say that the Church taught me as well as I the Church. When I came here I was a novice in Church discipline, I lacked experience and enthusiasm in Sunday-schools, I knew nothing practically of the details of an active city pastorate. I addressed myself honestly to the task before me, to do what I could; and I found difficulties lightened, and rough places made plain. The Church, instead of leaning on me, bore up my hands, bore with my obvious imperfections, and rallied to their young Pastor in his immense work with a unanimity which was itself a sure token of success. And the Lord granted his blessing abundantly. At almost every monthly communion some received the right hand of fellowship, and in a few months a gracious revival began, in which about a hundred were baptized.

Soon, among the numerous members on Church and Union Hills, regular prayer-meetings were established, and occasional preaching, resulting finally in the dismissal of many excellent brethren and sisters to constitute Leigh Street Church.

It was not long before the effort for the endowment of Richmond College demanded earnest co-operation with the Agent, Brother A. M. Poindexter, and many weeks of toil were given to aid him in that work, resulting in a contribution of some twenty thousand dollars at that time from this Church.

Scarcely had this been accomplished, when the same spirit of enterprise prompted the establishment of a kindred institution for young ladies. The Richmond Female Institute grew out of the consultations and efforts of a body of liberal and far-seeing brethren, in 1853, called together at the instance of Brother James Thomas, Jr. Though the Richmond churches had contributed that year about seven thousand dollars towards the erection of the new Church on Leigh Street, and nearly forty thousand dollars the year before to Richmond College, they pressed forward to this new enterprise with such zeal, that within a year they had the satisfaction of seeing the Richmond Female Institute opened, and the amplest facilities offered which an expenditure of some seventy thousand dollars in grounds, buildings, furniture, and apparatus could procure for the thorough education of our daughters.

To this new enterprise, which from the beginning had engaged much of my attention, I myself was unexpectedly summoned, after we had failed to obtain the Principal to whom our minds had been first directed. Finding my health failing under the pressure of manifold labors, and yielding to the advice and solicitations of such honored co-laborers as Jeter, Howell, the Thomases, Ryland, Goddin, and others, I assented to the change.

Visiting the Institute the other day, I amused myself by telling the young ladies, that I wanted to see if there was *as much beauty* there, as used to be in my day. And then gravely surveying their smiling, blushing, mirthful faces, I assured them that I was compelled to say that *there was not!* The explanation of this apparently ungallant speech was forestalled by the promptitude and quick wit of the accomplished Principal, Miss Hamner, who quietly said, "Dr. Manly means that there is not as much beauty, because there are not so many girls." "Precisely," I replied, "and there is good reason, in the changed circumstances, why there could not be expected as many now as then."

But may I be allowed to say it?—as I looked upon that fair group of lovely girls, my mind went back to the others who sat in those places twenty-five years ago; and the affectionate greeting, which my heart gave to the Institute Girls, was warmed and sweetened, along with a tinge of mysterious sadness, by the recollection of faces now beneath the sod. Were there ever any such girls any where as those that gathered there?

Yes, for their daughters and sisters are springing up all around us. Thank God for the blessed young people that are coming up to take the places of the old.—I should like to summon the teachers of those days around us again. One of the noblest has passed away, Prof. R. P. Latham; but Dr. H. H. Tucker still lives, full of labors and honors, and Dr. R. A. Lewis, and Prof. C. H. Winston, and Mrs. Holcombe, and Miss Lizzie Nelson, and Misses Jane Stanard, and Mary Lathrop, and Josephine Ragland. Bless them every one, wherever they are!

But I must not protract these reminiscences. Let us look forward rather than backward. This is the end of one century; let it be the starting point of new progress for the next. Serving our own generation by the will of God is the noblest honor to which we can attain. Serving, not being served, is the true dignity of man, and entitles one to the most enduring and the most illustrious memorial.

We need be little concerned about what posterity may say of us. The course of conduct which most effectively secures present usefulness will also ensure future influence; and if men erect no monuments to honor our names, that matters not. God will remember the work we tried to do, the work we wanted to do for him, the work that we did so imperfectly and feebly that we were ashamed at the time, and can scarcely now recall it without a painful sense of short-comings and deficiencies. But it was FOR HIM. That gave sweetness to the work then. That gives glory and permanence to it now. "Therefore, my beloved brethren, be ye steadfast, unmovable, always abounding in the work of the Lord, forasmuch as ye know that your labor is not in vain in the Lord."

ADDRESS

By E. W. WARREN.

WE are here in response to the call of our venerable mother.

Though only an adopted son, yet, having received such tokens of affection, and enjoyed so frequently the attention and warmth of love due only to the children, I claim the right, with them, to bring my grateful tribute, which is cordial and unaffected.

But few mothers have lived to so great an age. Not many have been permitted to call together their sons and daughters to rejoice in the celebration of their one hundredth birthday. We look into this maternal face, whose peaceful smile and tender greeting have so often given comfort and encouragement in the sorrows and strifes of life, and there remains still the beauty of youth gracing her brow, and increased elasticity, giving zest to her enterprises.

Her natural force is unabated, and her promise for another hundred years of activity and fruitfulness is a thousand-fold greater than when she began her life of consecration a century ago.

Her sons have come from afar to do her honor. Ardent and efficient reapers have, for the time, left their sickles in the midst of ripening harvests, and come to pay tribute of love to their spiritual Alma Mater. Her sons and daughters dispersed over the States of this Union, who are unable to be present at this happy family reunion, turning their hearts toward her, are saying: "For my brethren and companions' sakes, I will now say, peace be within thee." We, whose good fortune it is to be here, "Were glad when they said unto us, let us go up to this house of the Lord." Our hearts united in spiritual harmony as we united in the ancient chorus, "Our feet shall stand within thy gates," O thou blessed "Jerusalem." Journeying hither, as in visions we saw her in the distance, we unitedly cried: "Beautiful for situation, the joy" of all her sons and daughters, is this Zion of our spiritual nativity.

Now that we stand before these sacred altars, in the midst of these familiar scenes, and surrounded by this loving brotherhood, grateful memories of the past fill the mind, and as we are reminded of the wonderful achievements of the providence and grace of God in this place, and through this people, we exclaim with Jacob and Israel: "What hath God wrought!" As we enjoy the ever increasing fruits of these gracious agencies, we are in harmony with the sentiment of Moses; "Let thy work appear unto thy servants, and thy glory unto their children."

We are happy in this presence, and language refuses to express the fulness of love and joy we now experience. Looking into the faces of the many godly men and women who are here, we find reason to "thank God and take courage." Here sits our venerable brother (Dr. R. Ryland) who, as a minister, gave much of the strength of his vigorous manhood to sowing the precious seeds of eternal life; and as an educator, to preparing our people for that higher and broader culture, which is now so generally appreciated. He was the first *President* of Richmond College. He is to-day apparently as full of strength in body, of energy in intellect, of force in expression; as warm in heart, as loving in nature, as ever in the past.

Here, too, is our learned Gamaliel (Dr. B. Manly) in the vigor of manhood; every where regarded with "affectionate veneration," for his wisdom and piety. As happy in his explications of whatever is intricate, as he is felicitous in enforcing whatever is practical, or transparent in his expositions of whatever is polemic in theology. At his feet are gathering the consecrated young Timothys from the Southern States, that they may "learn the way of the Lord more perfectly," and understand better how to bear glad tidings of salvation to all the people.

Here, also, is our beloved Paul (Dr. J. L. Burrows)—not "the aged," for he never grows old—in the full stature of spiritual manhood. Matured in mental culture, with his Addisonian tastes and instincts. His much learning has not made him mad. He continues to speak forth the words of truth and soberness, with such force in argument, grace in style, and unction of the Spirit, that Felix trembles and Agrippa is almost persuaded to be a Christian.

> "We venerate the man whose heart is warm,
> Whose hands are pure, whose doctrine and whose life
> Coincident, exhibit lucid proof
> That he is honest in the sacred calling."

And also, here is our Apollos (Dr. J. B.

Hawthorne). "An eloquent man, and mighty in the scriptures:" combining in the proclamation of his sacred message, the graces of elocution, the vigor of thought, and the strength of argument. On every side we greet the well-trained, consecrated, laborious sons, from whose successful toil in other fields, numerous sheaves are being gathered for the heavenly garner. We greatly rejoice in their success; and bid them God speed in their glorious life-work.

Here, in generous sympathy with our joyous hearts, are our invited guests. It is sweet to feel we are all one in Christ. One in doctrine, one in hope, one in labor, one in destiny. That we are now permitted to dwell together in unity.

Before me are the familiar forms and faces of the Stephens and Philips, who are always ready, "as they have opportunity, to do good unto all men, especially unto them who are of the household of faith." Having used the office of a Deacon well, they "have purchased to themselves a good degree, and great boldness in the faith which is in Jesus Christ."

Seated on the pews before me, are the Phebes, the Priscillas, and the Marys. The faithful servants of the Church, who have bestowed much labor on it. They are still waiting before the sacred altars, with hearts and hands ever ready, saying: "Lord, what wilt thou have me to do?" They constitute an element of wonderful power, beginning now, as they were in the days of the apostles, to be appreciated and encouraged.

Here are we, in the midst of a godly brotherhood, who uniformly have a mind to work. Having laid hold on eternal life, they are fighting the good fight of faith. They are building up the walls over against their own houses, while they are going forth bearing precious seed. They are keeping the unity of the Spirit in the bond of peace, and are dwelling together in unity. "Behold, how good and how pleasant."

But I look in vain for forms and faces once familiar here. I listen for, but do not hear, the voices which once so lovingly imparted good cheer and wise counsel. Where are they? Did they not hear this call to fraternal reunion? Have they gone in response to an invitation to the family gathering above? Where are Morris and Courtney and Bryce and Kerr and Hinton and Jeter, once the loved, honored and successful pastors of this fold? Where are Broaddus and Keeling and Jennett and Taylor, who stood for a time in their lot as watchmen on these walls?

Where are the godly men and women, whose consecrated lives, whose religious intelligence, whose pious influence gave character and tone to the holy zeal and inspiration which to-day move us onward in our great mission of glorifying Christ and blessing humanity? They were lent to us for a season, that they might point towards heaven, and lead the way. Now they "rest from their labors, and their works do follow them." On their brows sit the "crowns of righteousness" which were reserved for them. They have gone to behold the glory of the Son which he had with the Father. They fought a good fight, they kept the faith, they have finished their course. They have entered into the joy of their Lord.

It is probable that one hundred years from to-day the members of this Church will gather here to celebrate its Second Centennial. Not one now present will be here to witness the joyous proceedings of that occasion. For one hundred years the members of this Church have been gathering to our "home over there." Every month of the year witnesses the departure of one or more. The voice still calls. It will continue to sound; and sooner or later it will be personal to each of us. The mansions are being prepared, they are almost ready for some of us. Soon the announcement will be made to us by him who has gone to prepare them, "Come, for all things are ready."

This is a pleasant reunion, but that will be infinitely more so. I anticipated this with pleasure; I look forward to that with joy. Here is only a part of the family; all will be there. Tears and sighs are here; fulness of joy will be there. We shall soon separate here, perhaps to meet no more till we pass over the other side; there we shall go no more out forever. Here we have mixtures of joy and sorrow, because of sin; there we shall be of the "spirits of the just made perfect." Here are vacant seats, and broken links, and aching hearts; there the loved and lost are found, the tears are dried, and death has gone forever. Here we are exiles from our Father's face, and our heavenly home; there we shall be "forever with the Lord."

> "Here in the body pent,
>   Absent from him I roam,
> Yet nightly pitch my moving tent,
>   A day's march nearer home."

Now we pant after God; then we shall be satisfied. Now we hunger and thirst after righteousness; then we shall be filled. Now we are members of the church militant and are pressing onward; soon we shall come to "Mount Zion, and unto the city of the living God, the heavenly Jerusalem, and unto an innumerable company of angels, to the general assembly and church of the first born, which are written in heaven, and to God, the judge of all, and to the spirits of just men made perfect, and to Jesus, the Mediator of the new covenant."

We will rejoice and be glad, for great is our reward of grace in heaven.

ADDRESS

BY H. McDONALD.

BRETHREN and sisters of the First Church: I congratulate you on this, the glad centennial of your Church. You are honored in that so many of your former Pastors are here to greet you. Here is Dr. Manly, who served you with his young and noble manhood. I was once his Pastor. I am sure he was more helpful to me than I was to him; here is Dr. Burrows, who seems to have lived with the Church all through her life from the fulness of fellowship and accuracy of detail with which he portrayed her noble history; but the years have gone over him lightly; he will always be young; here also is our beloved Warren, whose stay with us drew all hearts to him and whose withdrawment made us so sad only to make Georgia rejoice in the return of her noble son; here too is your present young and gifted

Pastor, the worthy successor of these beloved brethren. Accept my congratulations for the large, harmonious membership which fills these pews, and whose labors in all Christian work deserve unstinted praise. Thanks be unto God for all these.

What shall we say as our hearts have been so deeply moved at the mention of the former Pastors, whose labors are ended and whose is the everlasting rest? Morris, and Courtney, and Kerr, and Hinton, and Jeter whose name makes every lip tremble—what a noble galaxy in the firmament of heaven! Besides these, how many that once filled these pews, and whose hearts and voices praised the Lord of all, have gone to join the church of the first born in heaven? All honor and praise to God for this noble vine!

We come to-day from the churches that surround you; and, as children, we call you blessed. Nearly four years ago I came from Kentucky. My heart was heavy as I left her noble and ever dear people; but when I reached Richmond and received such a glad welcome from my own beloved Second Church, the pang of separation gave way to the joy of such hearty kindness. I thank you to-day for the grace and beauty with which you trained your daughters. With such a mother, how could they be otherwise than graceful and noble? With such a history of constant endeavor and gracious success, need we urge you to cherish deepest gratitude to God? Not by might or by power, but by his Spirit has all this been done. His hand led you from the feeble band of fourteen that organized on Union Hill to your present strength of numbers and efficiency. Let such mercies be recorded in the joy and praises of your heart and life. Let every heart and hand raise an Ebenezer to the God and Father of our Lord Jesus Christ.

With our gratitude for the past and present, let confidence and hope lead and brighten the future. Let the centennial upon which we now enter be as the one we close, only much more abundant for the glory of Christ and the good of men. With your hearts stirred by the gladsome memories of the holy living of the men and women who labored wisely and well in the past, let us turn to him who gave all, and anew let us give ourselves to him for work or sacrifice, as infinite love and wisdom direct. So be it; so be it!

SERMON.

BY

T. T. EATON.

SERMON.

"Be ye therefore perfect, even as your Father which is in heaven is perfect."—Matt. v. 48.

THOSE who have spoken to you so eloquently and well for the past two days, have told you of what God hath wrought in and through this Church during the century of its existence. They have recalled for you the past; I come to point you to the future, and to hold up before you a noble aim for which to strive—"Be ye therefore perfect, even as your Father which is in heaven is perfect."

No people have ever risen to greatness who did not place before their youth some ideal for which to strive. The ideal may never be realized; it would not deserve the name if it could be fully reached: but it is the point toward which all struggle, the model after which each man strives most earnestly. Show me what the ideal of any nation is, and I can tell you, to a great extent, the character of that people. And one of the most important duties of rulers and teachers of men is to erect some noble standard by which all shall be judged, and praised or blamed, as they approximate or deviate from it. Glance with me over the history of the world, and see the ideals of the nations, the results which followed their adoption, and the inherent defects in each. The great problem has ever been to make man perfect as is possible—to reach the highest stature of perfected manhood. And the difference is only in what constitutes true manhood, and the means by which it is to be attained. You may be very sure that there can be no noble nation whose ideal does not contain *some* of the qualities necessary to a perfected manhood.

The ideal of the Greeks was one of perfect beauty—physical beauty primarily, and in this their success was what we might expect to find. No people ever lived who carried their physical frame to such a height of perfection as did the Greeks. They studied and obeyed the great laws which govern health and beauty; they encouraged strength and grace by every means in their power, making their crowns, for skill in games requiring strength and agility, an honor and a glory, for which men sought earnestly;

and placing before their young men and maidens the perfection of physical beauty, in the statues of their divinities, as models to be imitated and reached, if possible.

As a natural result, no nation of earth has ever reached so high a type of physical beauty. To this day, amid the dwarfed, maimed, stunted bodies of men around us, our sculptors and painters can find no ideal for manly beauty or womanly grace, but are compelled to study the works of Phidias, Zeuxis, and other ancient artists; and we can find no higher comparison than to say of a face or a figure: "It is as beautiful as a Greek statue." They strove, too, for mental and moral beauty, as well as for that of the body, but with less success. There were far-reaching laws of mind and spirit which they could not grasp so readily as the physical laws. They laid down noble systems, but did not place before their youth those systems embodied in concrete forms.

Physically, the beauty of Apollo was flawless; morally, the character of the god was far from perfect manhood. The results upon the young could not fail to be disastrous; and the Greeks grew by degrees too much devoted to physical beauty, in which they excelled, and moral strength dwindled, while mental effort was confined too much to subtle disquisitions; and their nation fell before the Roman power. Their ideal was not perfect; but, such as it was, they reached it as no other people have ever done, and stand alone, high types of physical beauty, which, desirable indeed, is far from constituting perfect manhood.

The ideal of manliness among the Romans was one of courage and obedience to law—two most noble and essential traits of character, which made a great nation out of scattered bands of robbers. The world seldom sees such soldiers as these iron men, reared from their childhood to see all disgrace in cowardice and insubordination, and all honor in bravery and discipline. The models placed for the imitation of Roman youth were that Brutus, who in obedience to the majesty of law, condemned his own sons to the death they deserved, and saw the penalty inflicted without a falter; and that embodiment of courage, Horatius, who faced the enemy that had defeated the entire army in the field, and fought their whole force without one thought for his own safety, so only he could make his life last for the struggle till the bridge was down and the city saved. Discipline and courage! no wonder men led by such an ideal conquered the whole world. Our earth has never seen a nobler race of men, as a race, than those old Roman patricians, who welded all Italy into a sword for the world's conquest, and made it the proudest of boasts, "I am a Roman citizen"—a boast even an inspired Apostle was glad to make. And as we look back upon their nobility and greatness, we sigh to think that their obedience could not have been directed to the law of God, and their courage against the evil in the world, rather than against Gauls and Germans. Since their ideal had two great virtues, it made of them a great people, and in these points for which they strove they surpassed all other nations, as the Greeks did in beauty. As their ideal was defective, so in time it failed them: the courage of the old Romans became cruelty and brutality, their discipline made them obedient, not to righteous law, rightly enacted, but to the command of any victorious general who led their legions; and, when thus their ideal was changed and lowered, their national life went with it, and Rome became but the garnished sepulchre of her ancient greatness.

Two ideals swayed Europe during the Middle Ages, the monk and the knight. Evil as have been the results of the monastery, there was in the institution originally a great truth, or it would never have gained the hold upon the world which it possessed. Falsehood is weak; no system entirely false could control men's lives; and the great systems of false religion have succeeded, not because of their falsity, but because of the truth that was in them, which bore up their falsehood and made it powerful and dangerous. There was an essential element of true manhood in the ideal of the monk, however many errors were mingled with his theology, and however mistaken the means by which he sought to reach that ideal. The monastery was founded upon the great necessity of keeping in subjection the body with its passions and appetites—a necessity I fear we heed too little in these days, erring as far upon one side as the monk erred upon the other. For be assured the Apostle Paul meant something more than idle declamation, when he bade Christians to "crucify the flesh." It is the Holy Spirit that classes "the flesh" with "the world," and "the devil," as one of the three great enemies alike of piety and high manhood. One of Paul's greatest fears was lest, failing to keep under his body, he should be found to have fought in vain. "The lust of the flesh" is one of the chief sources of sin, and indeed all through the Epistles no duty is oftener or more earnestly enforced upon Christians than that of crucifying the flesh. Now crucifixion is not passive, but active; not the mere denial of gratification, but the actual infliction of suffering, and this is what the old monks strove to do. It is no delight in suffering or crucifixion which makes a merciful and loving Saviour give such harsh orders about the flesh, but that it is a great tempter of the soul. How many of the sins of which we are guilty—I mean outward sins and not evil tendencies—would a disembodied spirit have no temptation to commit? Take our bodies from us to-day, and all human legal enactments would be useless, all the second table of the law would pass away with the temptation to violate it. The ideal of the monks was right in the point of the necessity for crucifying the flesh, but wrong in the means they used to reach that desirable end—but, believe me, God will honor more their honest effort to keep the body in subjection, than, the modern refusal to crucify it at all.

The sins are legion which come from overfeeding or too high feeding of the body, and there is no more powerful defense against their attacks, nothing of greater avail in lessening their power, than the great duty of fasting, so often practised by Christ and the Apostles, so much considered a matter of course, that Jesus says, "when ye fast," as he says, "when ye pray," as if these were two duties his people would not think of omitting, and they therefore needed direction how to perform them acceptably rather than a commandment to do them. I fear, in this great duty of fasting, the churches are shamefully remiss, and the consequences of their failure are wide-spread over the earth today. Every commandment hath its peculiar blessing—its virtue, which it is designed to promote, and which can be accomplished by obedience to it, and it alone. This duty of crucifying the body hath its blessing of purity, to be attained in no other way, and uncleanness rules pampered bodies with a power which is well nigh irresistible. The Greeks gave their youth simple food and frequent fasts, in order to ensure to them that physical beauty which was their ideal. The Romans did the same, that they might be brave to endure hardship as well as to face danger, and strong to be conquerors and rulers of their own propensities, that no passion should interfere with their obedience to law. Shall Christians, with nobler aims, do less?

The monkish ideal was right on this point—right, too, in seeking to conquer fleshly lusts by simple food and fasting; but wrong, when, going beyond this, they strove to weaken muscular power as well as evil desires. They had their reward, however, in the success they achieved. Their orders spread rapidly over Europe, and their efforts to convert the heathen to at least as true a religion as they themselves knew, succeeded as no subsequent efforts of men bearing a purer doctrine have ever done. They had great strength to labor—great powers of endurance and a stern imperviousness to many temptations, which they would never have had but for the ideal they followed. What was wealth to a man whose clothing was rough hair garments, who wore no ornaments, owned no house to adorn, and ate only the cheapest food? Bribery of such men was impossible. For them, avarice had no power; luxury, no charms; and poverty, no terror. So long as they were true to their ideal, so long the truth that was in it brought its reward; and as we read their history we sigh to think that they should not have loved and served God, instead of the Pope; prayed to Christ, instead of to images and the Virgin; believed in justification by faith, instead of absolution at priestly hands; and learned the great lesson of crucifying the body out in the world, bearing a man's part and doing a man's work for the souls of men, instead of flying from the battle-field to hermitage and monastery. But their ideal was imperfect; carried too far, it overthrew itself in the scourging and nail-wearing which became unendurable; and in the rebound, they ceased from their fight against the flesh, gave up their simple diet and homely vestments, and became corrupt and corrupting. The light that was in them, from obedience to that one commandment, became darkness; and how great that darkness was, let their after history tell us.

While the monks placed before themselves the ideal of spiritual power, strengthened by overcoming the flesh, the laymen strove to reach the knightly ideal, the noblest of all which man has ever invented—nay, which would have been impossible to man alone, and has borrowed its noblest features from the oracles of God. The ideal of chivalry was courage, mercy, truth, and fidelity, founded on faith and obedience; and the results of this ideal, when acting upon noble natures, are seen in the characters of Bayard and Sydney. Fourteen years of his life the young knight spent in learning that great foundation lesson—obedience; and with it humility, in the menial services he must perform as page and squire. All through his course, religious duties were his constant portion, and dependence on God was strictly inculcated. And to be generous and merciful was as much a duty and a glory as to be brave and renowned in war. To have succored the needy, relieved the suffering, and freed the oppressed, made a man as honorable as to have captured a city, or routed an army.

The face of Europe changed under the power of this ideal: cruelty became an object of blame rather than of praise; self-sacrificing devotion took the place of selfish rapacity as an object to be striven for by the young. It was a useless and wicked waste of time and treasure and blood to endeavor to drive the Turks out of Palestine; but he was a far nobler man who left his home and its comforts behind him to go into a distant land to encounter certain danger and probable death in his love and reverence for the tomb of Christ, than the man who has indeed no Paynim blood upon his hands, but whose life is spent in money-making and self-aggrandizement. The knightly ideal was shadowed, alas, by the blighting errors of the Papacy, and flawed by its too great faith in physical blows and the power of the sword. But in spite of these great errors, it was a glorious model for the youth of Europe, and brought forth fruits which we are enjoying to-day. But as their ideal faded before their eyes, pride took the place of humility, and poverty became riches, and the knights became in their turn oppressors. Then the institution of chivalry became a jest and a reproach, to be buried with their unwieldy armor and their stately courtesy; not, however, until its grand ideal had perished, and the spirit had passed away, leaving the dead body of an empty pageantry.

If you will study closely the history of the world, you will find, as I said in the beginning, that every living nation must have its ideal; that it will surely rise in those virtues with which it invests its ideal of true manhood; that a noble people form for themselves ever a noble ideal, however, they may err in the means they use to bring their youth to that standard. It is an ignoble people which has a base ideal; and a hopeless people which has none; and when the ideal is set aside or lowered it is an unmistakable symptom of national decay and death. No matter how wealthy and prosperous, in seeming, the nation may be, corruption has begun; the tree of life is hollow-hearted, notwithstanding all the brave show of foliage it puts forth.

In ancient and medieval times, it is easy to see what was the object men set themselves to strive for; and, under all this imagined excellence, we find that the controlling purpose was to make humanity perfect. Man was himself the highest end; to raise the race to greatness and nobility was the purpose of all their effort. They differed in their ideas of what would accomplish this great purpose of human perfection. The Greek strove to make of man an Apollo; the Roman, a soldier; the medieval, a monk or knight; but the central thought with each was to make man perfect.

Now, turning our eyes from the past to the present, let us see what is the ideal before our people. What is the standard they have established for which their young men are to strive? I do not ask, what ideal they should have, nor what they profess to have; just as I did not take the ideals of the Greeks and Romans from the theories of their philosophers or the dreams of their poets; but what is the type of manhood, which in reality is most honored in the world to-day.

The first thing which strikes us as we look into the actual lives of the nations, is that the foundation principle has been changed; the central thought is no more to make man perfect, but to make imperfect man comfortable. There is the diameter of the moral universe between these two ideas. The more you think of them, the more closely you examine them in every point, and consider the influence they have upon the race, the more clearly you will see how antagonistic they are. Which is the grander motive for action? Which is the nobler desire—to be perfect, or to be comfortable? I do not contend that the ancients and medievals made men perfect—nay, they fell far short of it; but that was the object for which they strove—the ideal they placed before their youth. Neither can it be claimed that the moderns have made men comfortable,—for never was the race more restless; but only that is the ideal excellence for which they are striving. It is to be remembered, just here, that no nation ever rises higher than its ideal; and imagine, if you can, the results which must follow from the change which modern practicalness has made in the object of endeavor. Observe, also, that the modern does not object to any perfection which does not interfere with comfort, nor did the ancient object to any comfort which did not interfere with perfection, only the primary idea of the latter was to make man perfect, and of the former to make imperfect man comfortable.

And what are the means to be used to acquire this comfort? What is the ideal man whom we must imitate? To be comfortable, one must have money; the ideal man is he who can make it most rapidly. Everything which does not conduce to this great end is deemed visionary, impractical, and wanting in common sense. This ideal has infected the schools, and teaches the youth that education is to be made entirely subservient to "getting on in the world;" that, no matter how much certain studies may improve and elevate the intellect, they must be omitted if they can be turned to no commercial value afterwards; for that the object of an education is not to make the mind perfect as is possible, but to teach the man to make money, that he may be comfortable. Is not the world to-day one race-course, in which the prize is a purse? Here and there a man like Agassiz is found to refuse to join such a race, to answer an offer which would have brought him wealth, "Gentlemen, I have not time to make money;" but they are sneered at as visionary enthusiasts, as not up with the age, and as the Don Quixotes of modern society. If we were required to give a concrete form to the great ideals of the nations, would we not say, Theseus for the Greek, Brutus for the Roman, Hugo of Lincoln and Bayard for the medieval, A. T. Stewart and Cornelius Vanderbilt for the modern? In most sorrowful earnestness is not this true? And if the nobility of the nations is tested by the ideals they follow, how in point of manhood shall we rank this generation, in spite of its material comforts and modern improvements? Look honestly through all the smoke of the incense this age has burned to its own glorification, through the halo of vanity which surrounds its boasted progress; close your ears to the pæans it is singing to its own greatness and power, and decide calmly as to the nobility of its aims, and the true value of the comfort for which it strives.

" For we throw acclamations of self-thanking, self-admiring,
  With, at every mile—'run faster—oh, the wondrous, wondrous age!'
  Little thinking if we work our SOULS as nobly as our iron,
  Or if angels will commend us at the goal of pilgrimage.

" If we trod the deeps of ocean, if we struck the stars in rising,
  If we wrapped the globe intensely with one hot electric breath,
  'T were but power within our tether, no new spirit power comprising,
  And in life we were not greater men, nor nobler men in death."

There is the ideal for which we should strive—to be greater men in life and nobler men in death. But we can never be great or noble, until we place before us a noble standard of manhood, and strive with our might to bring ourselves and our race to that standard. Here is the great work which the churches owe to the world to-day; it is a work which must be done if the life of the nations is to be saved, and there is no power, save in the churches of Christ, from which there is any hope of health. Men must be given a higher ideal; it were far better that they go back to those former ages than continue to follow the ideal now set before them. If we must be idolaters, Apollo and Mars are nobler divinities than Plutus. But there is no need to return to those imperfect standards, deep as is the need of quitting the worship of Mammon and ceasing to find our highest type of manhood in Dives, Demas, and Simon Magus. We have in the Bible an ideal, as far above the money-making one, as heaven is above the earth—"Be ye therefore perfect, even as your Father which is in heaven is perfect." The ancients were right then in their central thought; the Scriptures side with them, that it is better and nobler to make man perfect than to make imperfect man comfortable; but they tell us, as Greek wisdom and Roman law could not do, how to make man perfect.

"As your Father which is in heaven is perfect." There, brethren, is the ideal to place before ourselves and the world. We shall never reach it,—it is a poor ideal which can be reached,—but what, think you, would be the effect upon the world if every man strove honestly to become like God? Man was made in God's image, is the finite representation of his infinite qualities. God made man upright, and the perfection of manhood is to abandon the "many inventions" man has sought out, and seek again to be a true image of the Almighty. This is the ideal, brethren, which we must substitute for the ignoble one men are now striving to reach. And we must impress upon the world that to seek this resemblance to God is not only the duty of the Christian, but the glory of him who is striving for true manhood;—that to be a *man* involves necessarily this resemblance to God. Begin in your own hearts and in your own homes. Do not let your children grow up thinking they may indulge in sin and pursue selfishly this modern ideal of the money-loving world, till they become Christians, and that then the Holy Spirit will change them. Teach them that all sin and all selfishness degrade their manhood; that apart from religion, all that is highest and noblest in them calls on them to be honorable and truthful, pure and self-sacrificing.

We boast of the wonderful progress the world has made in a century; of our machinery; our inventions and discoveries; and of our improved facilities, which our fathers lacked. During the past two days you have heard, told in eloquent language, of the great progress this Church has made in the hundred years of its history, and I would join my thanksgiving with yours for all that God has done in and through this noble band of Christians: but, after all, the question comes—Are we better men and women than those who lived a century ago? Do all our improved processes and facilities give the world nobler and holier people than those who laid the foundations on which we are building? This is the great question before us; it is the one measure of real progress.

It is not possible for humanity to stand still; placed as it is, between the beasts and God, it must either become more beastly or more godlike. And nothing is more beastly in its tendency than the ideal of comfort, or, as it is sometimes put, "to have a good time," as the object of life. This ideal is debasing and degrading beyond the power of language to express. There is not a swine wallowing in the mire in all the earth that is not doing all he can, "to have a good time;" and if this is the aim of a man's life wherein is he essentially better than a swine, for all the greater variety of food and occupation within his reach? Oh! brethren, let us rise above the swine, who care nothing for the perfection of swinehood, so their food is abundant and their sty comfortable. And I beg of you as a Church, to take this perfection of the Father which we are bidden to imitate—take his justice, his mercy, his wisdom, his truth, his holiness, and his love, as revealed in Christ Jesus our Lord, and hold them up as an ideal before the world, so that all men may strive to reach that standard, because it is the embodiment of all that is great and noble and lofty within the reach of humanity. A grand work this, for the Churches of Christ, but a work we can never accomplish —never!—by simply telling men "here is a noble ideal for *you* to follow." Greek and Roman, monk and knight, did not simply advocate their ideals for the rest of the world; they would only have excited contempt, and no one would have believed that their pretended admiration was anything but a farce;—but they strove themselves to reach their ideals. And men will never be moved, save to derision for our hypocrisy, if we plead with them to be perfect as our Father in heaven is perfect, and are not ourselves putting forth every exertion to reach as near as possible to that perfection. Oh! brethren, if we fail to do this; if our lives show that our words are empty mockery; if God receives our lips and Mammon our hearts and hands; if we too honor the man who is successful in business, and look with contempt upon such men as Agassiz who have no time to make money; if we agree that the great object is not to make man perfect, but to make him comfortable, giving gain the preference over nobility, heroism, and self-sacrifice, what will become of the world? If the light that is in the earth be darkness, how great is that darkness!

You stand a band nine hundred strong. If Christ's words abide in you, with greater strength and better opportunities than your fathers had, your achievements will be more glorious and far-reaching. Go forward then, brethren, step by step; so do armies march, so are victories won. This whole Church fighting bravely for Jesus would be a grand, soul-stirring sight. Take courage to-night, from the past God has given you,—from the opportunities that are present,—from the promises for the future which the Bible offers you. Resolve that every year, till you lay your armor down, shall see you living nearer to God, growing purer and purer, truer and truer, stronger and stronger in his service; and this Church ever advancing, ever victorious, shall look forth over the strongholds of sin cast down, the walls of error fallen, the powers of darkness beaten, and she shall be seen, by all who look upon her forward march in her strength and beauty, "fair as the moon, clear as the sun and terrible as an army with banners."

EXTEMPORE ADDRESSES.

BY

THOS. HUME, Jr.,
W. H. WILLIAMS,
J. WM. JONES,
J. B. HAWTHORNE, Pastor.

ADDRESS.

By THOMAS HUME, Jr.

I AM happy to answer this unexpected call and pay the unstudied tribute of a grateful heart amidst the common rejoicing. A "declaration of love" is nothing, if not personal. I need not, then, ask your indulgence for saying that, when, a boy of fifteen, I left my home for Richmond College, this Church and its school were the chosen haunts of my soul. I found a warm place in the family of the devoted man of God (Dr. Robt. Ryland), who is here, crowned with our reverence and love, the same serenely brave, patient, single-eyed champion of truth and righteousness he ever was; and afterward the tender watch-care of another household of faith (Deacon Richard Reins') cheered my heart and steadied my steps. Your cordial hospitality everywhere took me by the hand. God blessed and strengthened me through the rich associations it was my privilege to form, and many a noble type of character stamped itself on the sensitive young nature.

Such a training-school was it for many of us, in Christian experience, in church duties, in general religious plans, that no wonder we "rise up and call you blessed" in having blessed those who are to minister to others. All about us are humble workers who have accepted your generous invitation to this high festival, and who thank you for the inspiration it imparts. We will go back to our narrower fields of duty re-animated against depression; and, when tempted to grow weary in well-doing, the memory of your victorious review will keep off the sense of isolation and breed a healthful *esprit de corps* in the worn soldier. We feel that you belong to us as Christians, as Baptists, that we too are of that vast sacramental host of which you form so honorable and useful a part. We turn our believing gaze to the shining height on which your enterprise and devotion have planted our standard and struggle upward with undampened ardor.

Who was not comforted as he listened to the roll-call of worthies who "fought a good fight and kept the faith, "traveling on life's common way in cheerful godliness?" We saw that every kind of work and workman is needed and used by the Master, and the beautiful record of devoted laymen, some of them with no great fame in the outer world, but whose names are in the Lamb's book of life, both challenges our admiration and nerves us to take fresh heart of grace. Amid the apathy of professed followers of Christ, and the coldness and despair of a sneering materialism, their springing hope, their exceptional purity, their fidelity to principle, their deathless influence, gleams forth as the indestructible evidence of our Christianity; and we say, as we study their career: "This is the victory that overcometh the world, even faith."

> "Oh, though oft depressed and lonely,
> All our fears are laid aside,
> If we but remember only
> Such as these have lived and died."

It is well, honored Pastor and friends, that the key-note of to-night's services was struck by the noble sermon on the Christian Ideal. Memory is dear, but Hope still dearer. You have been reciting your history. You are to go forward now to make new history. The life of the believer and the Church has more to do with that which is to come. "It is good," as

Robertson says, "to have had a glorious Past; far better to have a glorious Future." This hundred-year old mother is vigorous and flourishing. The fresh life-blood pouring into her veins is ever renewing her youth. With a new Pastor you take a new departure, and will win new fruitful fields for Jesus, our King. Amongst the swelling tide of congratulations bearing prayer and hope to the Centenary feast, amongst your smiles and tears, I thank you that I am permitted to pour my libation on your shrine and bid you good cheer.

ADDRESS.

By W. H. WILLIAMS.

THE Pastor has just announced that the closing exercise of this interesting occasion would consist of "declarations of love" from some of the young men. I thank him for this manner of introduction. Had I been thus unexpectedly called upon for "a speech," I should have felt it my duty to decline. But it would be ungrateful in me to hesitate to declare my affection for my Mother Church.

No man living has greater reason to love her than I. Here, in early childhood, I first heard the sound of the preacher's voice. When too small to understand scarcely anything that was said, I was brought here. Well do I remember that when my mother sometimes quietly restrained me from whispering in church, my childish spirit rebelled, because the preacher, Dr. Jeter, could talk as much as he chose, while

I was not permitted to say a word. From that time onward this church has been interwoven with many of the most sacred experiences of my life. Around this building do the sweetest and saddest memories cluster.

In a little room, in what was then the rear of the church, on a certain Saturday night, at a Young Men's Prayer Meeting, conducted, I think, by John McCarthy, I first found peace in believing. I recall the new delight with which, on the next morning, I worshipped in this very room, while with happy heart I repeated a thousand times, the passage, "the love of Christ constraineth us." Here I was baptized by our brother, B. Manly, Jr., who is now with us. On the spot where I now stand, I was solemnly ordained to the work of the gospel ministry. The charge, solemn and impressive and still remembered, was delivered by our lamented Dr. Jeter, whose speaking portrait is here before you.

As I look over the congregation to-night, memory fills many of these seats with loved forms which are no more. Just there is the family pew. In imagination I see it occupied by father, mother, and other dear ones, who are now sleeping in Hollywood.

I remember, too, the young men of the church. There was true and noble George Leftwich, who cheerfully sacrificed the brightest prospects and even life itself at the call of duty. And there, too, was Harrison Watkins, who not long since exchanged the active duties of a vigorous Christian manhood for the rest of heaven. Ah! how would these, and many others who might be mentioned, rejoice in these sacred festivities!

We have been charmed with the delightful music rendered during this Celebration. But even now sweet melodies of other days come stealing back to my ears. You well remember how, at the close of our communion seasons, when new members had been received, James C. Crane used to step out of his pew over there, and with hymn-book in hand, and tear in eye, would walk down the aisle to the front, and, giving his hand to every newly-received member, sing:

> "Come in thou blessed of the Lord," with the chorus,
> "We welcome thee with one accord
> Our friends, our brethren."

Never until I reach heaven do I expect to hear music which shall thrill my soul more thoroughly than did that.

One element of strength in the Church has not been mentioned. She has ever given her young men cordial sympathy, and she has been wonderfully successful in awakening their enthusiastic attachment.

I remember seasons of perplexity when my burdens were lightened and my duty made plain by the sympathy and counsel of older brethren. In many of our churches there is an impassable gulf between the older and younger members. It was never so here. There has always been in this Church a number of brethren, more advanced in life, whom the younger members have regarded with filial confidence and affection. To this fact I attribute largely the success of the Church. God grant that this state of things may continue.

At this very hour there are men all over the face of the earth, who, because of past delightful association, turn with tender interest to this Church. For her they never cease to pray. When she weeps their tears flow, and when she rejoices they are filled with delight.

I beg you brethren, do not forget, in your prayers the young men you have sent forth. Surely, the mother will not be unmindful of her sons.

With such memories crowding upon me, my heart overflows with love to this dear Church, and my tongue refuses to utter all I feel.

I love to think of the future of this Church. A hundred years of her history have been completed. I cannot tell her coming struggles, but I may forecast her final triumph. The "Old First Church," with her long line of sons and daughters, shall join with the heavenly host in the grand chorus, "Worthy is the Lamb." Should I be numbered among that blessed assembly, not least of all will I thank God for such spiritual ancestry as he has given me, and while I live on earth I shall never cease to pray, "God bless my dear old Mother Church!"

ADDRESS.

By J. WILLIAM JONES.

I HAVE been quietly enjoying the exercises of this grand Centennial, with no expectation that I should be honored with even the humblest part in the programme.

But since I am thus called on I esteem it a privilege to be permitted to stand on this platform to express the very great pleasure I have had in all of these exercises—to congratulate this noble old Church on the splendid success of her Celebration—and to express the fond hope, and fervent prayer that her glorious past may be but the earnest of a yet more glorious future during the century she has just entered.

While it has never been my lot to be in any way connected with this Church, it has been my privilege, within the past few years, to minister somewhat frequently in her pulpit, to join in her worship, and to mingle with her membership. Having thus some opportunity of knowing the Church, I have been struck by *the harmony of feeling*—the unity of purpose—the concert of action—which seems so pre-eminently to characterize the membership. They sometimes differ, of course, as to measures, and have in their meetings warm discussions, in which each individual expresses his opinion with the emphasis and independence which is the glory of our Baptist faith. But, when the Church has once decided, it is beautiful to witness the spirit of concession and fraternal kindness in which the opposing parties *come* together, and *stand* together, and *work* together "in the unity of the Spirit and the bond of peace"—for the good of the Church and the glory of God.

And this same is true of the Baptists of Richmond and of Virginia. It has been long a subject of remark, that among the Baptist Pastors of Richmond and of Virginia there has been no petty jealousy, no unseemly rivalry, no discordant differences, but a personal affection, a loving sympathy, and a hearty co-operation, as beautiful as it has been promotive of the advancement of the cause we love.

In his able address on the "Deceased Pastors of the Church," Dr. Thomas remarked on the harmony and affection which existed between old Father Courtney and his Assistant Pastors. And in his admirable address last night Dr. Hatcher remarked on the power and influence which the old First Church has always had in giving tone to the spirit, and shaping the policy and plans of the Baptists of Richmond and of Virginia. Now who shall say how far this spirit of harmony is due to those grand old men who struck the key-note years ago, and left an impress on the Church which has influenced the Baptists of Richmond and of Virginia, and brought about the state of fraternity which we witness, and for which we thank God to-day?

Blessed spirit of harmony and peace! Blessed Church that has promoted it! May it continue, and widen, and deepen, as the years of the next century go on!

CONCLUDING ADDRESS

BY J. B. HAWTHORNE, Pastor.

WE have reached the conclusion of this celebration. For two days we have communed with the past. We have heard with grateful hearts the story of God's dealings with our fathers. We have seen how from extreme feebleness we have risen to great power. Enriched by the wisdom, and inspired by the examples of those who have gone before us in the good fight of faith, let us now turn our thoughts upon the future. Time past is past forever. It can never serve us again.

> "Listen to the water-mill all the live-long day,
> How the creaking of the wheels wears the hours away!
> Languidly the water glides ceaseless on and still,
> Never coming back again to the water-mill!
> And a proverb haunts my mind as the spell is cast—
> The mill will never grind again
> With the water that is past."

Let it be our purpose and ambition to make

the most of that part of life which is before us; let us crowd into it all that we possibly can of service to God, and of good to man. Let us bequeath to posterity as rich a legacy as has been left to us.

III.

SUPPLEMENTARY STATISTICS
AND
STATEMENTS.

SUPPLEMENT.

FINANCES AND PROPERTY.

FORMERLY the Finances of the Church were conducted by the Deacons. At present, all monetary interests, except the funds for the poor, are managed by a Finance Committee. The income of the Church is acquired by pew-rents, and by voluntary contributions in envelopes every Sunday morning and night. The collections of eight Sunday mornings in the year are devoted to benevolent objects, which are stated on the envelopes of the days assigned for these objects respectively. The current expenses of the Church are some seven thousand dollars per annum. This sum seems relatively large, as $3950 is reported as the yearly charities—for Missions and the poor. But, the church-books indicate only a small part of the donations of the Church. Scores of thousands of dollars are known to have been given by members of the Church to various benevolent objects, of which there is no record, except in the courts of heaven. The present Finance Committee are: John C. Williams, A. P. Fox, Charles T. Davis, Robert W. Powers, Patrick H. Starke, Peter W. Grubbs, John G. Spotts, John A. Belvin.

In compliance with the laws of Virginia, the property of the Church is vested in a Board of Trustees, as follows:

R. H. Bosher, James Thomas, Jr., Christopher Walthall, Coleman Wortham, John C. Stanard, R. W. Powers, Josiah Ryland.

POOR OF THE CHURCH.

The fund for the poor is raised by a monthly collection, at each communion season, and a general annual collection. Deacon Wm. G. Dandridge, Treasurer of this fund, has furnished the following paper:

> The Church recognizes distinctly her obligation to care for Christ's poor. About seven hundred and fifty dollars are annually appropriated to this purpose. The distribution is made mostly in money; sometimes in provisions; and chiefly by the Deacons. But valuable aid in this direction is afforded by the ladies individually and through their societies.
>
> Districts are assigned to the Deacons, who visit the poor within their limits, systematically. Members of the Church,

especially the ladies, also visit certain persons, of the poor, in whom they take a special interest. There are about twenty poor members of the Church who are more or less constant recipients of her bounty.

That the benefactions of the Church may be bestowed only on the disabled and really needy, all practicable caution and inquiry are employed in the dispensation of alms. The beneficiaries of the fund are, therefore, generally worthy persons and deserving of charity. Miss Lucy Courtney, a granddaughter of Rev. John Courtney, one of our former beloved Pastors, has been for many years blind and deaf. These infirmities, with advancing age, utterly incapacitate her for self-support. Hence she has, for a long period, gratefully and meritoriously received the cheerful support of the Church. She is a Christian of deep piety, and genial, submissive spirit, evincing a lively interest in the welfare of the Church, to which she is much attached. Visitors to the lonely room of this afflicted yet joyous saint, have often magnified God's sustaining grace, and bidden her farewell with suffused eyes and confirmed faith. She is eighty-eight years old.

The Church accepts the assurance of her Saviour that she will always have the poor with her; and that what she does unto one of the least of his little ones will be regarded as done unto him.

LIBRARY, INFANT CLASS, AND OFFICERS OF SUNDAY-SCHOOL.

In a recent refitting of the Sunday-school Rooms, with fountains and other improvements for health and ornamentation, the Library Department was enlarged, reorganized, and beautified. It is now a model as to convenience of arrangement and facility for distributing and preserving the books. The school is indebted for re-systematizing and improvement mainly to Mr. Carlton McCarthy, the Librarian of the School.

The Infant Class has been called "the pet" of the school. The ensuing notes are provided by the late Assistant Superintendent of the school, Deacon A. P. Fox:

"The Infant Class was organized in January or February of 1859, by Mrs. Abby M. Gwathmey. At first, there were twelve pupils. The number increasing, the class was divided. Mrs. Gwathmey retained the girls, and C. P. Burruss took charge of the boys. In the month of June, on account of the sickness of Mrs. Gwathmey, the entire class was put under the care of Mr. Burruss. Under his direction the average attendance was about twenty pupils. He was succeeded by William Forbes, under whom the children numbered between twenty and forty. E. Gathright had a fuller class. Mrs. Mary W. Curry followed Mr. Gathright, and has had charge of the class for some ten or twelve years. Under her administration it has been very prosperous.

There have been as many as two hundred children present. The average attendance is one hundred and twenty. "The Side Chapel" was built in the fall of 1871, for the accommodation of this school. The little ones are thoroughly drilled, and carry with them into the main school a good foundation of Scripture information for their future teachers to build on. In the absence of Mrs. Curry in Europe, the class is conducted skilfully and successfully by Miss Kate S. Winston, daughter of Professor Charles H. Winston, of Richmond College. Besides the above named teachers, others have taught well for a limited time.

The full corps of officers of the Sunday-school is as follows:

Wm. M. Turpin,	Superintendent.
D. S. McCarthy,	Assistant Superintendent.
Robert S. Bosher,	Secretary.
Geo. A. Haynes,	Assistant Secretary.
Carlton McCarthy,	Librarian.
A. L. Haynes,	Assistant Librarian.
N. B. Pleasants,	do do
A. B. Tyree,	do do
E. C. Walthall,	do do
W. A. Barrett,	do do
Willie Reins,	do do
Josiah Ryland,	Treasurer.
Geo. A. Hundley,	Collector.
Jacob Reinhardt,	Organist.

Officers and teachers	60
Scholars	525
Average attendance of scholars	337
Volumes in library	847

YOUNG MEN'S PRAYER-MEETING.

This meeting is one of the fixed and best institutions of the Church. A brother writes: "It is difficult, indeed impossible, to estimate its value to the young brotherhood." The following sketch is from Deacon R. H. Bosher:

> The completion and dedication of the new Church edifice, in October, 1841, infused into the membership a very decided progressive spirit. There were a number of prominent and pious brethren ready to every good word and work, but so modest and shrinking that the energies of the Church were not fully developed.

Our special need was a pious, gifted, and active man, possessing the affection and confidence of the Church, to take the lead in its various enterprises and activities. The return to the city of Brother James C. Crane, and his connection with the Church supplied in an eminent degree this need.

He came at once to the front, and with all his noble gifts and energies, devoted himself to the service of his Master in bringing to light the buried talents of his servants.

Among other valuable suggestions of Brother Crane, was that of a Young Men's Prayer-Meeting, which was immediately adopted, and put into practice.

The first Saturday night in January, 1842, was appointed to begin this meeting. Six brethren, assembled in answer to this call, namely: Wm. Tyree, Wm. G. Dandridge, J. L. Apperson, Geo. J. Hooper, J. W. Meanley and R. H. Bosher.

The meeting was a decided success from its start; many of our brethren who had not participated in the Prayer and Conference Meetings of the Church connected themselves with it. Some of them were advanced in life and others of middle age. They were punctual and constant in their attendance, and contributed, by prayers, exhortations, and example, to its success.

Among those of this class who have passed away and whose names are fragrant in the memory of this meeting, may be mentioned, Wm. Tyree, Henry Keeling, R. L. Coleman, Chas. Wortham, Wm. Beale, John C. Franklin, Geo. W. Atkinson, James C. Spotts, G. R. Myers, Jas. H. Walthall, Albert G. Wortham, R. B. Tyler and others.

Of those who died in early life were Saml. C. Clopton, Wm. M. Gaskins, Geo. W. Keesee, Geo. M. Leftwich, Wm. Ligon, David R. Crane, John H. McCarthy, Henry M. Walthall, Edward S. McCarthy, James T. Crane.

From the organization of the meeting, no portion of our membership have aided the Pastors more largely in all special and protracted efforts; and no other agency of the Church has been more potent in developing the gifts and piety of our young brethren.

In its infancy, the Pastors, Deacons, and indeed many of our older brethren took a lively interest in its prosperity; and were frequent in their attendance, exhorting and bidding our young men God-speed.

This meeting has been constantly held during thirty-eight years past, even while our city was besieged, and the roar of guns was heard. Those that have enjoyed its privileges appreciate them to some extent. But all that it has accomplished we can only know, when we join our loved ones in that better land.

LAST HALF DECADE OF THE CHURCH.

Dr. Burrows' "History of the Church," properly closes its details with the year 1874. Something should be said of the Church and its Ministry since that time.

For six months the Church was ably supplied by Dr. J. L. M. Curry, assisted by a brother-minister of the church. The Church would have unanimously numbered Dr. Curry among its Pastors, but he prevented the proposed invitation to its pastorate. For some three months, Rev. Duncan McGregor, of England, preached; and was subsequently "called" *for twelve months.* The call was not accepted.

Rev. E. W. Warren, D. D., began his ministry here in March, 1876, and closed it on the second Lord's Day in October, 1879. At the "Centennial" he said that Dr. Burrows was the Paul, and Dr. Hawthorne the Apollos of the

Church. What name would better suit himself than the John of the "Old First?" In an Autograph Album, presented to him the day after the celebration by the "Young Ladies' Missionary Society," the writer noticed these inscriptions: "A good Minister of Jesus Christ;" "Blessed are the pure in heart, for they shall see God."

Having referred to this "Presentation," which took place in the "Side Chapel," it may not be amiss to remark, that our good brother showed himself capable of saying pleasant with wise things on a pleasant occasion. A set of Resolutions had been previously sent him. From his reply, on receiving the Album, we copy these words: "In the Resolutions I received, you sent me the *heart* of the Society. In this beautiful Autograph Album, just presented through my beloved brother, Dr. Tupper, and which I accept with feelings of profound gratitude, you give me your several *names*, with many choice sentiments and loving wishes for my future usefulness and happiness. I bear in my *own heart* the *photograph* of each of you. So, having your heart, your names, and your photographs, I shall henceforth enjoy the privilege of being the rich possessor in its entirety of 'The Young

Ladies' Missionary Society of the First Baptist Church of Richmond.'"

The speech was tender and loving—much in the vein of John, when he wrote: "The elder unto the elect lady and her children, whom I love in the truth * * and now I beseech thee, lady, not as though I wrote a new commandment unto thee, but that which we had from the beginning, that we love one another. And this is love, that we walk after his commandments."

The following summary of his work in Richmond appeared in the *Religious Herald* of October 23d, 1879.

Not to praise him, but to tell what Dr. E. W. Warren has done in Richmond, and the spirit that moved him, as Pastor of the First Baptist Church, is the object of this article.

In the spring of 1876, he succeeded Dr. Burrows, now of Kentucky, a man cultivated, eloquent, successful, and pious. It took a *man* to fill his place. The congregations did not diminish under the change, but on Wednesday and Sabbath evenings they grew in interest and numbers. The varied religious efforts of the membership suffered no detriment. All church work went forward with unimpaired vigor.

During Dr. Warren's charge, three extra, or protracted, meetings were held, in which he did most of the preaching and labor. Over one hundred happy converts and the quickening of the Church are some of the results of the earnest, precious meetings. While he was connected with the Church, one hundred and thirty-four persons were received by baptism. If due allowance is made for diminutions by removals, and erasures or "dropping" on account of unknown residence, the increase of the roll strength of the Church may be fairly stated at one hundred and seventy-five. The Young Men's Missionary Society of the Church has grown in zeal and activity. It supports a laborer in the State Mission field, and contributes annually three hundred dollars to the Baptist German City Mission. The Ladies' Missionary Societies are also doing a noble work. One of them supports a native Chinese missionary, and the other assumes five hundrd dollars of the support of Miss Stein, our accepted missionary to China. The Sunday-school continues large, flourishing, and efficient. The poor, sick, and bereaved have been tenderly cared for, and in his nine hundred annual pastoral visits, all hearts in our families have been won by the light and love and warmth which Dr. Warren's presence diffused. Evidently all his powers were consecrated to the cause of the Master, and his teaching and pure example stimulated the graces and developed the Christian character of his flock.

* * * * * *

He leaves the Church full, strong, united, active. The Lord has given him success in Richmond, and the Church which he leaves declares that they will "part from him with sorrow, and he will bear to his new field their undivided love, and also their prayers for his greater usefulness." The saintly Payson advised a brother minister, "Paint Jesus Christ upon your canvass, and then hold him up to the people; but so hold him that not even your little finger can be seen." If our late beloved Pastor had been so advised, he could scarcely more fully have followed the counsel, for he literally hid himself behind the cross. A MEMBER.

Richmond, Va.

Rev. J. B. Hawthorne, D. D., entered upon the pastorate of the Church on the first Sunday in December, 1879. The congregations have been very large. After crowding every pew, the Ushers have had to send many away for lack of seats. The spectacle of the galleries packed with young men is often thrilling. A new feature of the congregation is the large number of our most intelligent colored people who attend the worship. God has blessed the preached word. In a series of special meetings, conducted by the Pastor with skill and power, some forty were added to the Church by baptism—among the number, his own and only two children. In the Church and congregation and community, there is felt in regard to the new Pastor much of enthusiasm.

Dr. Hawthorne has been elected on the Boards of Foreign Missions, Richmond College, and the Richmond Female Institute. In the last institution, he succeeds Dr. Jeter as its President. It may not be an unpardonable offence against delicacy to add that Mrs. Hawthorne has speedily captivated the hearts of the members of the Church.

The prosperity of the Church was never greater, if it is tested by the number and character of its membership, the attendance on the devotional services, the activity of the Societies and the Sunday-school, the attention to the sick and the poor, and the harmony and love of the "Conference Meeting."

In some respects, this last-named meeting is the most important of the Church. For the benefit of those who are unacquainted with the democratic polity of Baptist churches, each of which is independent, in government, of all other churches or church organizations, it may be stated that at this "Conference," as it is commonly called, all business of the Church is openly transacted. All candidates for membership, if they do not bring letters from other Baptist churches, are examined; and on satisfactory profession of their faith in the Lord Jesus, are accepted for baptism, which admits them to the Lord's Supper, before which they receive "the right hand of fellowship," in token of their full membership in this particular Church; all cases of discipline are reported and disposed of; all plans for church work are discussed and determined; all committees are appointed, and make their reports; and all officers of the Church are elected. To this meeting the Sunday-school, the Societies, and the Treasurers of the Church, make annual reports. This Conference is the Church in its organic and executive capacity. It has no legislative power; but it has the power derived from God's word, to enforce the laws of the Head of the Church on its own membership, which recognizes it as the highest ecclesiastical authority. At such a meeting there will naturally be diversity of opinions and sentiments and speech; but the voice of the majority is the decision of all questions. The spirit of the body is as conservative and harmonious as it has ever been during its long and distinguished career of harmony and conservatism. Its motto might well be the last text of the Pastor: "Faith, Hope, Charity—these three: but the greatest of these is Charity."

In this connection, and as the conclusion of this Memorial Volume, the following report, from the pen of James Thomas, Jr., Chairman of the Committee to nominate a Pastor, may be appropriately recorded:

"The Committee to whom you entrusted the important duty of nominating a suitable minister of the gospel for Pastor of this Church, have executed that duty to the best of their ability.

"We were guided in our decision by the past of this old Church,—now nearly one hundred years old,—the chief feature in whose long history has been its uniform harmony—having one heart, one mind, one way. Another marked feature has been the overflowing congregations of young as well as old, and the extraordinary additions to the membership, when the pulpit was filled by a preacher of great power and eloquence and zeal in winning men to Christ. From all we know and can learn of the Brother whose name we present, he can and, if obtained, will deepen and widen for the future these two main features in our past history, namely, brotherly love, and enlarged prosperity.

"We, therefore, unite unanimously in nominating Rev. J. B. Hawthorne, D. D., for Pastor of the First Baptist Church, with the earnest hope of his receiving the unanimous vote of the Church."

INDEX.

A

ABERNETHY, Alexander, 24, 25.
Agassiz, Louis, 312.
Allen, William, 145.
Alvey, Laura, 100
American Bap. Miss. Union, 217.
"America's Contribution to the Wealth of the World," by J. L. Burrows, D. D., 18.
Anderson, Jane L., 100.
Anderson, Rev. Peyton, 226.
Anthony, Rev. Joseph, 56.
Apperson, James L., Treas., 155, 181, 235, 342.
Apperson, Mary W., 99.
Arnold, Benedict, 48.
Associations Bapt., Culpeper, Va., 63.
  Dover, 55, 57, 70, 119, 120, 214, 220.
  Elkhorn, Ky., 62.
  General of Virginia, 20, 32, 61, 89.
  Licking, Anti-Missionary, Ky., 62.
Atkinson, Geo. W., 77, 97, 181, 342.

B

Bagby, A., 239.
Baker, Rev. Elijah, 56, 111.
Ball, Rev. Eli, 87, 272.
Baptist Preacher, 126.
Bargamin, Olivia, 100.
Barrett, W. A., 341.
Bayard, Chevalier, 307, 312.
Beale, Wm., 342.

Belvin, John A., 338.
Belvin, Mrs. John A., 238.
Benedict, David, D. D., 214, 215.
Berry, Miss Lelia, 239, 240.
Bibb, Ann L., 99.
Biblical Recorder, 80.
Blair, Rev. Mr., 67.
Blenner, Rev. John, 102.
Bodeker, H., 234.
Bosher, Mrs. Elizabeth, 76, 105.
Bosher, Mrs. E. J., 240.
Bosher, Mrs. Gabriella, 76.
Bosher, Georgie, 100.
Bosher, Robert H., Deacon, 12, 13, 38, 84, 156, 181, 183, 276, 341, 342.
Bosher, R. S., 234, 341.
Bosher, Miss Sophie, 240.
Bosher, William, 77.
Braine, Rev. Samuel, 70.
Braine, Rev. William, 70.
Braxton, Martha, 100.
Briel, Mr. Barney, 144.
Briel, Mrs. B., 144.
Broaddus, Rev. A., 17, 28, 29, 43, 57, 69, 125, 241, 288.
Broadus, John A., D. D., 244.
Brockenbrough, Miss Sallie, 224.
Brutus, 312.
Bryce, Rev. John, 29, 69, 123, 125, 225, 226, 241, 288.
Buchanan, Rev. John, 225.
Buchanon, Rev. John, 51, 66.
Burnett, James E., 98.

Burke, Virginia, 100.
Burress, Miss Georgia, 236.
Burrows, J. L., D. D., 13, 15, 18 21, 23,
  27, 28, 29, 30, 31, 160, 170, 191, 204,
  216, 221, 286, 292, 343 345.
Burrows, Mrs. J. L., 221, 224, 238.
Burrows, Rev. Lansing, 101.
Burruss, Mr. C. P., 340.
Butler, Frederick, 97.
Butler, Thomas, 98.

C

Callaham, Miss Willie, 236.
Campbell, Alexander, 75, 156.
Campbell, Rev. Duncan R , 86, 225.
Carey, Rev. Lott, miss'y, 221, 222.
Carey, William, D. D., 193.
Carrington, Mrs. Col., description of
  old Richmond, 51, 53.
Cary, Harriet, 99.
Cary, Howard H., 98.
Caster, Franklin, 98.
Caulfield, William, 97.
Chalkley, O. H., Deacon, 135.
Chamberlayne, Custis, 98.
Chandler, Christopher S., 98.
Charlton, Miss Jane C., 175, 176.
Chase, Irah, D. D., 125.
Chastaine, Rev. Rene, 61.
Chaucer, extract from, 67.
Childery, Stephen, 77.
Childs, Susan R. 99.
Choir, 24.
Churches, Baptist.
  Antioch, formerly Bear Swamp, 111,
    213.
  Beulah, King William Co., Va., 79.
  Blue Creek, Ky., 115.
  Blue Run, Orange Co., Va., 62.
  Boar Swamp, now Antioch, 111, 213.
  Bordentown, N. J., 77.
  Brashear's Creek, Ky., 114, 117.
  Broad Run, Fauquier Co., Va., 64.
  Buckingham, Va., 61.
  Bull Run, Fauquier Co., Va., 64.
  Cedar Creek, Ky , 116.

Chesterfield, 59.
Chickahominy, Va., 56.
Crocked Run, Culpeper Co , Va., 63.
Dover, Goochland Co., Va., 55.
Ebenezer, Richmond, 261.
Elk Creek, Ky., 115.
First African, Richmond, 81, 85, 86,
  225, 247.
First Richmond, 11, 28, 45.
  Constituent members of, 146.
  Members of, 1790, 1824, 68.
      " 1835, 77, 81.
      " 1842, 86.
      " 1849, 85.
      " 1854, 95.
      " 1874, 96.
  State in 1780 and 1880 compared,
    104.
Fouth, Richmond, 87.
Fox Run, Ky., 115.
Fulton, Richmond, 95, 225.
Georgetown, Kentucky, 87.
German Church, Richmond, 102.
Ghent, Ky., 116.
Goldsboro, N. C., 103.
Goochland, Va., 55.
Hicksford, Va., 103.
James City, Va., 111.
Jefferson, Ky., 113.
Leigh Street, Richmond, 91, 225.
Long Run, Ky., 115.
Lower King and Queen, Va., 58.
Lynchburg, Virginia, 87.
Manchester, 95, 102.
Manchester, African, 86.
Meherrin, Lunenburg Co , Va., 61.
Mill Creek, Ky., 116.
Moratico, Va., 58.
Mound Bluff, Miss , 87.
New Bridge, Va., 78.
New Hope, Wash. Co , Ky., 116.
New Market, or Fourth, Phil., 71.
Norfolk, Va., 125.
Nottaway, Va., 60.
Pine Street, Richmond; 95, 103.
Piscataway, Essex Co., Va., 58.
Port William, Ky., 116.

INDEX.

353

Powhatan, Va., 59.
Reeds, Caroline Co., Va., 58, 70.
Rehoboth, King William, Va., 57, 118.
Second Richmond, 72, 82, 86, 156, 158, 176.
Second African, Richmond, 86.
Severns Valley, now Elizabethtown, Ky., 116.
Sharon, King William Co., Va., 79.
Shelbyville, Ky, 117.
Sidney, Richmond, 91, 225.
Skinqnarter, Va., 59.
St. Stephens, King and Queen Co., Va., 78.
Third, or Grace Street, Richmond, 82, 86.
Tomahawk, Va., 59.
Upper King and Queen, Va., 57.
Venable Street, Richmond, 95, 159, 225.
Vernon, Miss., 87.
Clay, Rev. Eleazar, 59.
Clay, Henry, 55.
Clay, Rev. John, father of Henry Clay, 55.
Clopton, Betty, 100.
Clopton, Judge John B., 160.
Clopton, Maria G., 99.
Clopton, Rev. S. C., missionary, 88, 181, 232, 342.
Clopton, W. E., Deacon, 160.
Coghill, Miss Elizabeth, 176.
Coghill, Miss Susan, 176.
Coleman, R. L, 342.
Columbian College, 88, 125.
Commonwealth, Extract from, 33.
Compiler, Richmond, extract from, 34.
Connally, Mrs. J. K., 238.
Connolly, John, forfeited property of, 50.
Cornwallis, Lord 48.
Council, Rev. James G., 101, 181.
Courtney, Rev John, 28, 31, 57. 67, 68, 69, 72, 74, 75, 117 — 123, 216, 217, 226, 241, 288, 293, 332, 339.
Courtney, Miss Lucy, 275, 339.

Covington, Theo. Sem'y, 87.
Cowardin, Jas. A, Esq., 34.
Cowie, Agnes, 99.
Crnig, Rev. Lewis, 62,
Cram, James T., 341.
Crane, Isabella, 99.
Crane, James C., Deacon, 30, 84, 97, 166—70, 182, 221, 222, 223, 232, 241, 276, 327, 342.
Crane, David R., Church Clerk, 97, 156, 277, 342.
Crane, William, Deacon, 217, 218, 222, 223.
Crawford, H. J., 181.
Crawford, Mrs. T. P., 237, 239.
Crenshaw, Mrs. Winifred, 76, 99.
Cundiffe, Henry, 98.
Cunningham, Frank W., 24, 26.
Curry. Rev. J. L. M., LL. D, 12, 15, 24, 28, 30, 102, 187, 228, 242, 343.
Curry, Mrs. M. W., 340.

D

DABBS, Josiah, 97.
Dabney, Mrs. M. F., 236.
Dabney, William, 76, 175.
Dagg, John L, D D., 228.
Dandridge, Alphonzo, 98.
Dandridge, Elizabeth, 100.
Dandridge, Jane, 99.
Dandridge, Louisa, 100.
Dandridge, Spottswood M., 77.
Dandridge, Wm. G., Deacon, 12, 92, 155, 338, 342.
Daniel, Miss Jane, 176.
Daniels, Columbus A., 98.
Davenport, Rev. Robert, Miss'y., 181, 220, 232.
Davies, Rev Samuel, 70.
Davis, Chas. T., 338.
Davis, D. O., Church Clerk, 39, 155.
Davis, Mrs. D. O., 240.
Davis, John G., 178.
Dennis, Elizabeth, 99.
Diddep, Thomas, 146.

Dispatch, Richmond, 34.
Dodson, Rev. E., 29, 129.
Dorcas Society, 32, 235.
" Dover Decrees." 75.
Dudley, Rev. Ambrose, 62.
Durham, Sarah, 99.

E

EAGER, Rev. J. H., 14.
Eaton, T. T., D. D., 16, 33, 295.
Ellyson, Henry K., 226.
Ellyson, Onan, Deacon, 75, 157.
Evans, Susan M., 99.

F

FARRAR, John, Deacon, 30, 84, 97.
Farrar, Margaret, 100.
Farrar, Susan, 100.
Forbes, Wm., 340.
Ford, Pamelia, 100.
Ford, Rev. Reuben, 55.
Ford, Rev. Reuben, Junior, 91.
Ford, Virginia E., 100.
Foster, Mary P., 99.
Fox, A. P., Deacon, 12, 92, 155, 338.
Franklin, John, of Union Hill, 54, 111, 145, 146.
Franklin, John C., 342.
Franklin, William, 145, 146.
Frayser, Lewis, 225.
Frayser, Mrs Lewis, 224.
Frayser, William, Deacon, 30.
Frayser, William, Soldier, 98.
Freeman, John and Samuel, carpentering of church edifice by, 151.
Fristoe, Rev. Daniel, 63.
Fristoe, Rev. William, 63.
Frost—teacher in S. S., 178.
Fuller, Richard, D. D., 171, 193.
Furman Institute, S. C., 89.

G

GAINES, M. E. M., 99.
Gannaway, Eliza, 100.
Gardner, Elizabeth, 99.

Garnett, Rev. James, 63.
Garlick, Joseph R., D. D., 101.
Gaskill, Rev. Varay S., 89, 182.
Gaskins, Rev. Wm. M., 89, 96, 102, 184, 342.
Gates, General, 48.
Gathright, Mr. C., 240.
Gelbardt, Leon, M. D., 97.
General Assembly of Virginia, 52.
General Assoc. of Virginia, 20, 32, 89.
George, Rev. Z. Jeter, 96, 102.
Georgetown College, Ky., 90.
German Bap. City Mission, 348.
Girard College, 34.
Girls' Aid Society, 32.
Glenn, Thomas J., 75, 156.
Goddin, 279.
Goodall, Rev. John, 111.
Grant, Miss Sarah, 176.
Graves, Gen. Azariah, 126.
Gray, G., 239.
Green, General, 48.
Greenhow, Elizabeth H., 99.
Greenhow, Mrs. Frances, 175, 176.
Greenwood, Rev. James, 58.
Gregg, Rev. Jacob, 71.
Grubbs, Peter W., 338.
Gwathmey, Mrs. Abby M., 340.
Gwathmey, W. H., Deacon, 23, 92, 155, 233, 276.

H

HALL, Rev. Addison, 80.
Hall, Miss Henrietta, 181.
Halsey, Mrs., 121.
Hamner, Miss, 280.
Hardgrove, Mary W., 99.
Hardgrove, Samuel, 77, 97, 159, 249.
Hardgrove, Thomas, 77, 97.
Harris, Mary T., 100.
Harris, Rev. Samuel, "A Paul among the Churches," 61.
Harrison, Rev. Edmund, 102.
Harrison, Rev. John C., 77.
Harrison, Wm. L., 97.
Hart, John, Deacon, 155.

Hart, Rev. John, 102.
Hart, Rev. Wm. H., 226.
Harvey, Mrs. Samuel, 224.
Harwood, Wm. F., Deacon, 155.
Hatcher, Rev. Jeremiah, 59.
Hatcher, W. E., D. D., 15, 31, 204, 332.
Hawthorne, J. B., D. D., 12, 13, 20, 21, 22, 23, 29, 31, 105, 190, 242, 287, 333, 343, 346, 347.
Hawthorne, Mrs. J. B., 224, 347.
Haynes, A. L., 341.
Haynes, Geo. A., 341.
Haywood, Mrs., 146
Hendricks, Lewis C., 98.
Henson, P. S., D. D., 101, 182.
Herndon, Richard N., 180.
Herring, John H., 98.
Hickman, Rev. William, 59, 113, 114.
Hill, Miss Ida, 240.
Hill, Owen B., M. D., 97.
Hill, Wilson B., 77, 97.
Hillyard, Miss Bettie, 76.
Hillyard, John, 97.
Hillyard, Mrs. Mary E., 76, 224.
Hillyard, Miss Sarah, 175.
Hinton, Rev. Isaac Taylor, 28, 29, 81, 82, 133, 134, 242, 288, 293.
Hobson, Julius A., 97.
Hobson, Mrs. Julius A., 146.
Hodgen, Rev. Isaac, 116.
Hodge, M. D., D. D., 170.
Hoff, Edward H., 24, 25, 26.
Holcombe, Mrs., 281.
Hollins, Mrs. John, 121.
Holmes, Susanna, 99.
Hooker, Sarah V., 100.
Hooper, Geo. J., 342.
"House of one Franklin," 23, 28, 143-147, 213.
Howell, R. B. C., D. D., 279.
Hoyt, U. G., Deacon, 155.
Hudgens, Mattie Lee, 100.
Hudgens, Thomas S., 98.
Hudnall, Mrs. Henry, 274.
Hugo of Lincoln, 312.
Hume, Rev. Thomas, Jr., 32, 321.
Hundley, Geo. A., 341.

Hundley, Miss Sallie, 240.
Hurst, Rev. T., 72.
Hyde, Charles H., Deacon, 75, 157.
Hyde, Robert, Deacon, 75, 157.

I

IAGE, J. T., 98.
Ide, Geo. B., D. D., 37.
Imprisoned Baptist Ministers.
  Baker, Rev. Elijah, 56.
  Craig, Rev. Elijah, 62.
  Craig, Rev. Lewis, 62.
  Greenwood, Rev. James, 58.
  Ireland, Rev. James, 64.
  Marshall, Rev. Daniel, 57.
  Tinsley, Rev. David, 59.
  Ware, Rev. Robert, 58.
  Weatherford, Rev. John, 60.
  Webber, Rev. William, 55.
  Young, Rev. John, 58.

J

JEFFERSON, Thomas, 46.
  Life of by Tucker, 52.
Jefferson, the Sexton, 26.
Jennett, Rev. C. B., 28, 29, 138, 288.
Jeter, J. B., D. D., 17, 19, 28, 29, 31, 38, 82, 84, 85, 88, 118, 134—137, 188, 189, 198, 201, 204—208, 229, 231, 232, 241, 247, 251, 263, 267, 275, 288, 293, 325, 326, 347.
Jeter, Mrs. J. B., 89, 238.
"Jeter Memorial," 13, 20, 23, 31, 185—203.
Johns, Bishop, Episcopal, 263.
Johnson, teacher in S. S., 178.
Johnson, Miss America A., 236.
Johnson, Eleanor, 99.
Johnson, Elijah, 181.
Johnson, Rev. Francis C., 101.
Jones, J. William, D. D., 33, 330.
Jones, Martha T., 100.
Jude, Miss Kate, 236.
Judson, Mrs. Ann Haseltine, 225.
Judson Female Miss'y Soc., 224.

K

Kate, John B., 98.
Keeling, Rev. Henry, 28, 29, 69, 82, 96, 102, 125, 126, 176, 229, 232, 233, 241, 288, 342.
Keeling, Rev. Henry, Sr., 125.
Keesee, Rev. Geo. Wm., 103, 183, 342.
Keesee, Thomas W., 97.
"Kentucky, Baptists of," 113.
Kentucky County, divided, 49.
Kerr, Rev. John, 21, 28, 30, 73, 75, 76, 81, 105, 126—133, 139, 187, 196, 241, 288, 293.
  Extract of Sermon by, 130.
Kingsford, Edward, D. D., 89.
Kingsford, Mrs. Edward, 221.
King's Mountain, battle of, 48.
Knight, Mrs. C. T., 221.
Knight, Miss Sallie, 239.
Knowles, Mrs. John H., 24, 25.
Koontz, Rev. John, 64.

L

Lacy, C. E., 234.
Lafayette, General, 73.
Lanave—teacher in S. S., 178.
Lane, Rev. Dutton, 57.
Latham, Prof. R. P., 281.
Lathrop, Miss Mary, 281.
Lee, Aaron, anecdote of, 266.
Lee, General Henry, 48.
Lee, R. B. Treas., 155, 234.
Leftwich, Fannie W., 99.
Leftwich, George M., 98, 342.
Leftwich, Thomas 97.
Leigh, B. Watkins, 265.
Leland, Rev. John, 56.
Lewis, Mrs., constituent member of the Church, 146.
Lewis, F. I., Deacon, 76, 159.
Lewis, Dr. R. A., 281.
Lewis, Zachary, Deacon, 75, 159.
Liberia, Rev. E. Ball visits, 88.
Ligon, John L., 97.
Ligon, Miss S., 221.
Ligon, Wm., 342.

Lipscombe, Ella J., 100.
Lipcombe, Mary, 99.
Lomax, Rev. A A., 102.
Louisville, founded, 50.
Luck, Rev Julian M., 102.
Lunsford, Rev. Lewis, 58.
Lyell, Frances, 100.

M

Major, Rev. Richard, 64.
Manly, B., D. D., 14, 16, 19, 22, 28, 32, 90, 242, 275, 286, 292, 325.
Mann, Wm. P., 181.
Marion, General Francis, 48.
Marshall, Rev. Abraham, 216.
Marshall, Rev. Daniel, Missionary to Indians in Penn., 57, 216.
Marshall, Rev. Jacob, 79.
Marshall, Chief Justice, John, 63, 165.
Marshall, Mrs. Maria O., 175, 176.
Marshall, Col. Thomas, 64.
Marshall, Rev. William, uncle of Chief Justice Marshall, 63.
Mauzee, Miss Polly, 76, 99.
McCarthy, Carlton, 234, 325, 341.
McCarthy, D. S., 341.
McCarthy, Edward S., 342.
McCarthy, John H., Ch Clerk, 97, 156, 157, 342.
McCarthy, Julia A., 99.
McCurdy, Miss Kate, 240.
McDonald, H., D. D., 16, 32, 292.
McGregor, Rev. Duncan, 24, 343.
McKim, Robert, 76.
Meade, Bishop, Episcopal, Extract from his "Old Churches," 51.
Meanley, J. W., 341.
Meredith, Adaline, 100.
Meredith, Eliza, 100.
Meredith, Nannie, 100.
Minor, George A., 22.
Miller, Mrs. Martha, constituent member of Church, 146.
Moon, Miss Edmonia, missionary, 237, 238, 239.
Moon, Miss Lottie, missionary, 237, 239.
Moore, Bishop, Episcopal, 76.

INDEX.

Moore, Rev. Richard C., 226.
Mordecai, Mr , extract from Reminiscences of, 65.
Morris, Rev. Joshua, 12, 28, 29, 31, 50, 51, 65, 110—117, 214, 241, 293.
Murphy boys, 57.
Murray, Thomas, 145.
Murray, Mrs., 145.
Myers, G. R , 341.

N

NELSON, Miss Lizzie, 281.
Nelson, Miss Mary, 175.
Nelson, Peter, Deacon, 72, 75.
Newton Theological Seminary, 88.
Noel, Rev Theoderick, 57.
Norton, Rev. Rich. W., 101.
Norvell, Thomas B., 77.
Nowell, Miss Martha F., 176.

P

PAGE, Carter, 27.
Page, Mrs. Martha A., 221, 224.
Parrish, Royal, 77, 97.
Patterson, Margaret L., 100.
Patterson, R. F , 234.
Pearce, Mrs. Patience, 99.
Pearce, Miss S., 221.
Pegram, Gen. J. W., 158.
Phidias, proposed statue of Alexander, 199.
Philips, Miss Betsy, 177.
Phillips, Rev. Barnard, 78.
Pickens, General, 48.
Pickett, Rev. John, 63.
Pierson, Rev. Moses, 116.
Pleasants, N. B., 341.
Pleasants, Miss Nettie, (M. Antoinette) 239.
Pleasants, Miss Sue (Keziah) 239, 240.
Pleasants, U. B., 24. 25.
Plummer, W. S., D. D., 61.
Poindexter, A. M., D. D., 278.
Porter, Rev. Jeremiah B., 78.
Potts, John W , 98
Powel, Ann H., 99.

Powers, R. W , 13, 338.
Powers, Sidney, 97.
Powers, William, 97.
Princeton Theological Seminary, 80.
Programme of Celebration, 13-16.
  Musical, 25, 26.

Q

QUESENBERRY, Ella, 100.

R

RAGLAND, Miss Josephine, 281.
Ratcliffe, Miss Virginia, 76, 175, 176.
Read, Rev. Dr. A. W., 101.
Read, Peyton G., 98.
Redmond, Thomas C., 98.
Reinhardt, Prof. Jacob, 24. 341.
Reinhardt, Mrs. Jacob, 24, 25.
Reins, F. W., 235.
Reins, Miss Jane, 221.
Reins, Mrs. Jane F., 76.
Reins, Richard, Deacon, 30, 76, 84, 97, 161, 171, 249, 321.
Reins, Willie, 341.
Religious Herald, 27-33, 345, 246.
Religious Inquirer, 126.
Repiton, Rev. A. Paul, 80, 161.
Rice, Rev. John H., 67, 226.
Rice, Luther, D. D., 31, 161, 217, 218, 219, 223, 228, 229, 241, 242.
Richmond, Baptists in, 1780 and 1880, 104.
  Churches in, 1780, 1880, 104.
  Church members in, 1880, 104.
  Population of, 1780, 12, 104.
  Population of, 1880, 104.
Richmond, African Bap. Miss. Socy., 221, 222.
Richmond College, 23, 30, 82, 85, 88, 103 187, 202, 347.
Richmond Female Institute, 22, 30, 90, 188, 347.
Robards, Rev. Mr., 86.
Robertson, Rev. F. W , 193, 324.
Rogers, John, 98.
Rogers, Mary J., 99.

Roper, Rev. David, 73, 76, 79, 222, 226, 229.
Roper, George, 176, 229.
Roper, Miss Mary Frances, 79.
Ross, Miss Sarah, 175.
Ryland, Mrs. Callie T., 221.
Ryland, Carrie V., 100.
Ryland, Mrs. Josephine, 221.
Ryland, Josiah, 338, 341.
Ryland, Mrs. Josiah, 236.
Ryland, Robert, D. D., 15, 19, 28, 32, 81, 85, 103, 138, 233, 245, 256, 279, 285, 321.
Ryland, Mrs. R., 120.
Ryland, Rev. Wm. S., 101, 183.
Rutherford, Mrs. Laura, 236.

S

SADLER, R. S., Deacon, 155.
Sands, Rev. Alex. H., 101, 182.
Sands, J. H., 234.
Savage, Frances W., 98.
Scott, Nicholas, "Old Nick," 265.
Se:n Sang, Yong, 220.
Semple, R. B., D. D. 111, 112, 118, 119, 124, 214, 216, 229, 241.
"Sewing Circle" of First Church, 223.
Shelburne, Rev. James, 60.
Shepherd, Mrs. Ann M., 143.
Shockoe Mission, 234.
Shuck, Rev. J. L., Missionary, 70, 220, Marries Miss H. Hall, 181.
Sizer, James, Deacon, 30, 76, 162, 171, 178, 231, 249.
Sizer, Nancy, 99.
Slaughter, Edmonia, 100.
Smith, A. B., 233.
Smith, John D., 152.
Smith, Sarah Jane, 99.
Smith, Virginie B., 100.
Smither, Geo. W., 98.
Smither, John L., 97.
Snead, Rev. Herman, 70.
Southern Baptist Convention, 32, 213, 220.
Southern Baptist Theological Seminary, 30, 90, 188.

Southwood, Rev. Wm., 78.
Spare, Philip, 175.
Spencer, Rev. Dr., 111, 113, 117.
Spilman, Lucy, 100.
Spotts, James C., 97, 342.
Spotts, John G., 338.
Spotts, Mattie Lee, 99.
Stanard, Miss Jane, 2 6, 281.
Stanard, John C., Deacon, 84, 155, 338.
Stanard, Robert C., 98.
Starke, Ashton, 234.
Starke, Joseph, Deacon and Pastor, 76, 78, 159.
Starke, Mrs. M. T., 76.
Starke, Patrick H., 12, 338.
Starke, Thaddeus B., 97.
Staughton, Wm., D. D., 125, 228.
Steane, Martha, 99.
Stearns, Rev. Shubael, 57, 216.
Stein, Miss Sallie, Missionary, 239.
Stewart, A. T., 312.
St. John's Episcopal Church, Richmond, 51.
Straughan, Rev. Samuel L., 217, 241.
Sumner, George J., Deacon, 92, 155.
Sumter, General, 48.
Swedenborg, Baron, 269.
Sweeney Miss Mary, 236.
Sydney, Sir Philip, 307.

T

TAKE, Alvey, 151.
Talman, J. Sr., 233.
Tatum, Wm. H., Treas., 155.
Taylor, G. B., D. D., 215, 226.
Taylor, Isaac, English Author, 133.
Taylor, Rev. Isaac, 116.
Taylor, James B., D. D., 28, 73, 89, 138, 217, 242, 276, 288.
Taylor, Rev. John, 63.
Teage, Rev. Colin, Missionary 221, 222, 223.
Temple, James H., Deacon, 77, 160.
Temple, Mrs. J., 239.
Terrell, Agnes W., 100.
Theseus, 312.

Thomas, Archibald, Deacon, 30, 77, 164-166, 171, 179, 219, 231, 232, 241, 249, 276.
Thomas, Mrs. Archibald, 221.
Thomas, Mrs. Catharine, 76, 105.
Thomas, Rev. David, 64.
Thomas, James, Jr., 12, 178, 182, 241, 249, 277, 279, 338, 349.
Thomas, Mrs. James, Jr., 221, 224.
Thomas, Miss Mary Ella, 224.
Thomas, Rhoda, 99.
Thomas, W., D. D., 14, 21, 29, 69, 101, 183, 191, 214, 331.
Thomas, W. O., 183.
Thomas, Mrs. Wilson, 224.
Thompson, Herbert C., Clerk, 156.
  Supt. of S. S., 176.
  Ordained, 176.
Thompson Sarah C., 99.
Thornton, Anthony R., Deacon, 75, 279.
Thornwell, 193.
Tinsley, Rev. David, 59.
Tinsley, Rev. Jacob T., 79.
Tinsley, Rev. Thomas, 59.
Trowers, Thomas, 97.
Tucker, Dr. H. H., 281.
Tucker, Rev. W. H., M. D., 102.
Tupper, F., 234.
Tupper, H. A., D. D., 12, 13, 16, 28, 31, 38, 102, 344.
Tupper, Mrs. H. A., 221, 238.
Tupper, H. A., Jr., 183.
Tupper, P. Y., 235.
Turner, Rev. Jesse H., 226.
Turpin, John, 97.
Turpin, John L., 77.
Turpin, Rev. John O., 79, 101, 183.
Turpin, Mildred, 99.
Turpin, Rev. Miles, 88.
Turpin, Dr. Peter, 28, 66, 149, 150.
Turpin, Richard, 77.
Turpin, W. H., 13.
Turpin, W. M., 183, 341.
Tyack, Samuel, 97.
Tyler, Mrs., her account of the Franklin house, 143.
Tyler, J. P., Treasurer, 75, 155.
Tyler, R. B., 342.
Tyler, Washington, 98.
Tyree, A. B., 341.
Tyree, William, 77, 342.

U

UNIVERSITY of Virginia, 102, 103.

V

VALENTINE, John B., 13, 229.
Vanderbilt, Cornelius, 312.
Vardeman, Rev. Jeremiah, 116.
Vass, Rev. James L., 102.
Virginia, in 1780, 45.
  Agriculture in. 46.
  Dwellings in, 45.
  Manufactures of, 47.
  Traveling in, 47.
  Baptists in, 215.
Virginia Baptist Convention, 216.
"Virginia Baptists, History of," by Dr. R. B. Semple, 214.
"Virginia Baptist Ministers," by J. B. Taylor, D. D., 89, 217.
Virginia Baptist Seminary, removed, 82.
Virginia Education Society, 30, 187.
Virginia Foreign Miss. Soc., 31, 213, 217.

W

WALKER, Rev. Jeremiah, 59, 60.
Walker, L. D., 181.
Wallace, Rev. Isaiah T., 101, 224.
Waller, Rev. George, 116.
Waller, Rev. John, 62.
Waltars, J. B., Deacon, 92.
Walter, Thos. U., Architect of Church edifice, 34, 151.
Walthall, B. W., Deacon, 76, 139.
Walthall, C., Deacon, 14, 15, 22, 29, 30, 84, 155, 180, 181, 182, 231, 235, 338.
Walthall, E. C., 341.
Walthall, Mrs. Elizabeth, 76.
Walthall, Henry M., 342.

Walthall, James H., 97, 342.
Walthall, J. B., 234.
Walthall, Rev. Joseph S., 80, 102, 180.
Walthall, Madison, 75, 229.
Walthall, Mrs. Matilda, 221.
Walthall, S. H., 77.
Ward, Daniel, 97.
Ware, Rev. Robert, 58.
Warren, E. W., D. D., 15, 16, 19, 23, 29, 32, 105, 239, 242, 292, 343, 345.
Warren, Mrs. E. W , 224.
Warren, L. R., Deacon, 155.
Washington, General, in N. J., 48.
Watkins, H. H., 234.
Watkins, Rev. Henry W., 96, 103.
Watkins, John, 77, 97.
Watkins, J. B., Deacon, 14, 30, 155.
Wayland, Francis, D. D., 193.
Weatherford, Rev. John, 60.
Webber, Rev. Wm., 55.
Weller, D. and C. R., 152.
Wesleys, The, 193.
Wharton, Rev. Dr. M Bryan, 101.
Wheeler, Wm. J., 98.
White, Emeline, 99.
Whitefield, Rev. George, 55, 57, 193, 216.
Whitelock, James W., 98.
Wickham, William, 265.
Williams, Mrs. Elizabeth, married to Rev. John Kerr, 128.
Williams, Miss Emma, 76.
Williams, Jesse, 77, 151.
Williams, John, 146.
Williams, Rev. John, 60.
Williams, John C., Church Clerk 13, 155, 233, 338.
Williams Mary W., 100.
Williams, Miss Rebecca, 175.

Williams, Miss Susan, 146.
Williams, Rev. W. Harrison, 33, 101, 183, 325.
Williamson. Rev. George, 70.
Winfree, Ada B., 100.
Winfree, D. B., D. D., 23, 28.
Winston, Prof. Chas. H., 159, 281, **340**.
Winston, Miss Kate S., 340.
Winston, Peter, Deacon, 75, 158.
Winston, Mrs. P., 76.
Witt, Rev. Jesse, 89.
Woman's Miss. Socy. of Richmond, 32.
Woodfin, George, 229.
Woodson, Joseph, 178, 179.
Woodward. R. L., 235.
Wooldridge Charlotte, 99.
Wortham, Albert G., M.D., 97, 233, 342.
Wortham, Mrs. A. G., 221.
Wortham, Charles, 97, 342.
Wortham, Charles T., 233, 277.
Wortham, Coleman, 12, 276, 338.
Wortham, Miss Coleman, 221, 224.
Wortham, Edwin, 233.
Wortham, Mrs. Edwin, 224, 238.
Wortham, Mary, 99.
Wortham, Mary C., 100.
Wortham, Miss Mary T., 240.
Wortham, Richard C., 77, 97, 2 9.
Wortham, Mrs. R. C., 76.
Wright, Rev. John, 57.
Wyatt, Miss C. V., 24, 26.

Y

Yong Seen Sang, 220.
Young Ladies' Missionary Society, 32, 344.
Young Men's Missionary Society, 32, 346.
Young, Rev. John, 58, 118.

www.ingramcontent.com/pod-product-compliance
Lightning Source LLC
Chambersburg PA
CBHW020325240426
43673CB00039B/923